8TH GRADE ENGLISH AND LANGUAGE ARTS

Unit 4

Understanding Literary Texts

Table of Contents

Leadership 101

THOROUGHNESS

Knowing what factors will diminish the effectiveness of my work or words if neglected

ResponsiveEd® thanks Character First (www.characterfirst.com) for permission to integrate its character resources into this Unit.

Objectives

- Read grade-level texts with fluency and comprehension.
- Analyze, make inferences, and draw conclusions about theme and genre in literary texts.
- Analyze literary works that share similar themes across cultures.
- Analyze how the central characters' qualities influence the theme of a fictional work and resolution of the central conflict.
- Understand, make inferences, and draw conclusions about the structure and elements of fiction.
- Analyze plot developments to determine whether and how conflicts are resolved.
- Explain how the values and beliefs of particular characters are affected by the historical and cultural setting of a literary work.
- Analyze different forms of point of view, including limited versus omniscient, and subjective versus objective.
- Understand, make inferences, and draw conclusions about the structure and elements of poetry.
- Understand, make inferences, and draw conclusions about how an author's use of sensory language creates imagery in a literary text.
- Explain the effect of figurative language, such as similes and extended metaphors, on a literary text.
- Compare and contrast the purposes and characteristics of different poetic forms.
- Write poems using poetic techniques, figurative language, and graphic elements.
- Compare and contrast mythologies from various cultures.
- Apply knowledge of literary terms to a fictional work.

1. YOUR ROLE AS A READER

Objectives:

- Read grade-level texts with fluency and comprehension.
- Analyze, make inferences, and draw conclusions about theme and genre in literary texts.

Vocabulary:

comprehension – the process of understanding a text

genre *[ZHAHN-ruh]* – a category or style of something

inference *[IN-fer-uhns]* – a guess or speculation a reader makes based on the evidence given in a text

Have you ever considered your role and responsibilities as a reader? When you learned how to read, you learned how letters form words when they are put together a certain way. You learned how to pronounce words aloud. You learned that words have meaning. As you increased your skills as a reader, you learned that reading does not simply involve pronouncing words correctly and knowing what they mean.

Reading involves **comprehension**, or the process of understanding a text. Yes, you do need to know what the words you are reading mean; however, the process of reading is more involved. As a reader, you need to actively participate in your reading by gathering meaning from a text. A writer does not craft a text so that the person who reads it will just be able to understand each word of the text. A writer expects the reader to be able to understand the meaning of the text as a whole. In order to do so, the reader must actively form ideas about the text in his or her mind.

Making inferences is part of being an active reader. An **inference** is a guess or speculation a reader makes based on the evidence given in a text. Making inferences involves reading in between the lines of a text, and going beyond its stated meaning and trying to figure out what the writer wants you to conclude from the text.

Read the following passage and try to determine the meaning of the passage as a whole.

Thomas stared gloomily at Bailey, his childhood companion and faithful football buddy, who had done nothing but lay at the bottom of the stairs for a week now, letting out a sad whimper every so often. The food in his dish had remained untouched for a few days, and lately, he wouldn't even get up off the cool tile to greet Thomas when he came home from school.

"Mom, we have to do something for him. He looks so miserable," Thomas murmured.

"I think we've done everything we can do, Thomas. Even Dr. Miller said that, at this point, all we can do is make him as comfortable as possible. I'm sorry, honey."

In this passage, the author does not tell you exactly what's happening. Can you infer the meaning of the passage? You probably guessed from the details in the passage that Bailey is Thomas's dog, and that Bailey is very sick, but the author did not explicitly give you this information. Gathering meaning from details in a text is what making inferences is all about. Being an active reader will help you better understand the text you are reading.

Visualizing is another strategy you can use to aid comprehension. If a science textbook describes the bubbling and foaming of the chemical reaction of vinegar and baking soda, try to imagine what that looks like. In your mind's eye try to see the white bubbles foaming up in the container. Listen with your mind's ear to the sounds the bubbles make as they foam and pop. If a history book describes the conquistadores (Spanish explorers) landing in Florida, think about what Florida must have looked like. Think about what the conquistadores were looking for and what they found. The more you engage your senses as you read, the better you will understand and remember what you are reading.

GENRES OF LITERATURE

Understanding the genre of a text will also help you as you read it. A **genre** is a category or style of something—in this case, writing. You are likely familiar with genres of music, such as classical, pop, and rap. In the same way, genres of literature are different kinds of literary writing. In this Unit, you will learn about the genres of poetry and fiction. The category of poetry contains several subgenres, or categories of poems, such as lyric, narrative, and epic. Fiction contains subgenres such as historical fiction, mysteries, realistic fiction, and fantasy stories.

As you read, it is important to understand the genre of the text you are reading. You should read different genres with different purposes in mind. For example, most fiction stories have the purpose of entertaining the reader, while the purpose of most informational texts is to inform the reader. An editorial in the newspaper likely has the purpose of convincing the reader to accept a certain viewpoint. Many times, the purpose of a poem will be to evoke (draw out) a certain emotional response or reaction from the reader. Understanding the purpose of the literary work will help you in determining a purpose for reading the work. When reading a fiction story, you can read it for the purpose of being entertained. Making inferences and connecting with the text will help you to enjoy the story even more.

Review

Read the excerpt, making inferences as you read.

"Buck's Trial of Strength"
by Jack London

John Thornton, owner of the dog, Buck, had said that Buck could draw a sled loaded with one thousand pounds of flour. Another miner bet sixteen hundred dollars that he couldn't, and Thornton, though fearing it would be too much for Buck, was ashamed to refuse; so he let Buck try to draw a load that Matthewson's team of ten dogs had been hauling.

The team of ten dogs was unhitched, and Buck, with his own harness, was put into the sled. He had felt the general excitement, and he felt that in some way he must do a great thing for John Thornton. Murmurs of admiration at his splendid appearance went up. He was in perfect condition, without an ounce of superfluous [unnecessary] flesh, and the one hundred and fifty pounds that he weighed were so many pounds of grit and virility. His furry coat shone with the sheen of silk. Down the neck and across the shoulders, his mane, in repose as it was, half bristled and seemed to lift with every movement, as though excess of vigor made each particular hair alive and active. The great breast and heavy forelegs were no more than in proportion with the rest of the body, where the muscles showed in tight rolls underneath the skin. Men felt these muscles and proclaimed them hard as iron, and the odds went down two to one.

"Sir, sir," stuttered a member of the latest dynasty, a king of the Skookum Benches **[men who have become rich in the gold rush]**. "I offer you eight hundred for him, sir, before the test, sir; eight hundred just as he stands."

Thornton shook his head and stepped to Buck's side.

"You must stand off from him," Matthewson protested. "Free play and plenty of room."

The crowd fell silent; only could be heard the voices of the gamblers vainly offering two to one. Everybody acknowledged Buck a magnificent animal, but twenty fifty-pound sacks of flour bulked too large in their eyes for them to loosen their pouch-strings.

Thornton knelt down by Buck's side. He took his head into his two hands and rested cheek on cheek. He did not playfully shake him, as he was wont, or murmur soft love curses; but he whispered in his ear. "As you love me, Buck. As you love me," was what he whispered. Buck whined with suppressed eagerness.

The crowd was watching curiously. The affair was growing mysterious. It seemed like a conjuration **[a summoning of supernatural aid]**. As Thornton got to his feet, Buck seized his mittened hand between his jaws, pressing in with his teeth and releasing slowly, half-reluctantly. It was the answer, in terms, not of speech, but of love. Thornton stepped well back.

"Now, Buck," he said.

Buck tightened the traces, then slacked them for a matter of several inches. It was the way he had learned.

"Gee!" Thornton's voice rang out, sharp in the tense silence.

Buck swung to the right, ending the movement in a plunge that took up the slack, and, with a sudden jerk, arrested his one hundred and fifty pounds. The load quivered, and from under the runners arose a crisp crackling.

"Haw!" Thornton commanded.

Buck duplicated the maneuver, **[agile movement]** this time to the left. The crackling turned into a snapping, the sled pivoting and the runners slipping and grating several inches to the side.

The sled was broken out. Men were holding their breaths, intensely unconscious of the fact. "Now, Mush!"

Thornton's command cracked out like a pistol shot. Buck threw himself forward, tightening the traces with a jarring lunge. His whole body was gathered tightly together in a tremendous effort, the muscles writhing and knotting like live things under the silky fur. His great chest was low to the ground, his head forward and down, while his feet were flying like mad, the claws scarring the hard-packed snow in grooves. The sled swayed and trembled, half-started forward. One of his feet slipped, and one man groaned aloud. Then the sled lurched ahead in what appeared a rapid succession of jerks, though it really never came to a dead stop again—half an inch—an inch—two inches. The jerks became less as the sled gained momentum, he caught them up, till it was moving steadily along.

Men gasped and began to breathe again, unaware that for a moment they had ceased to breathe. Thornton was running behind, encouraging Buck with short, cheery words. The distance had been measured off, and as he neared the pile of firewood which marked the end of the hundred yards, a cheer began to grow and grow, which burst into a roar as he passed the firewood and halted at command. Every man was tearing himself loose, even Matthewson, who had lost his wager. Hats and mittens were flying in the air. Men were shaking hands, it did not matter with whom, and bubbling over in a general incoherent babel. But Thornton fell on his knees beside Buck. Head was against head, and he was shaking him back and forth.

"I'll give you a thousand for him, sir, a thousand," sputtered the Skookum Bench king, "twelve hundred, sir."

Thornton rose to his feet. His eyes were wet. The tears were streaming frankly down his cheeks. "Sir," he said to the Skookum Bench king, "no, sir. You can hold your tongue, sir. It's the best I can do for you, sir."

Buck seized Thornton's hand in his teeth. Thornton shook him back and forth. As though moved by a common feeling, the onlookers drew back to a respectful distance; nor did they again interrupt.

Choose the correct answers.

1.1) _____ What is the purpose of this story?
   A. to inform the reader about dogsledding
   B. to entertain the reader with a story about dogsledding
   C. to convince the reader that dogsledding is wrong
   D. to inform the reader about the dangers of betting

1.2) _____ What can you infer about Thornton from the first paragraph?
   A. He does not want to be humiliated by refusing a bet.
   B. He likes to bet.
   C. He believes that Buck can pull the sled with one thousand pounds of flour on it.
   D. He wants to sell Buck.

1.3) _____ What kind of relationship do Buck and Thornton have?
   A. Thornton is harsh with Buck.
   B. Buck does not like Thornton.
   C. Buck loves and respects Thornton.
   D. Thornton loves Buck, but Buck does not love Thornton.

1.4) _____ Why doesn't Thornton accept the Skookum Bench king's offer of $800 in exchange for Buck before the challenge begins?
   A. Thornton believes, without a doubt, that Buck can pull the sled.
   B. Other men pressure Thornton to participate in the bet.
   C. Thornton has never lost a bet.
   D. Thornton loves Buck and believes in him. He does not want to sell Buck.

1.5) _____ At what point in the story is the suspense highest?
   A. when Buck is unable to break the sled out of the ice
   B. when one of Buck's feet slips as he is trying to jerk the sled forward
   C. when Buck reaches the end of one hundred yards
   D. when Thornton refuses the offer of $1,200 for Buck

1.6) _____ How do the men react to the outcome of Buck's test?
- A. They are angry with Thornton for misleading them about Buck's strength.
- B. They are angry at having lost so much money on the bet.
- C. They are astonished and begin cheering for Buck.
- D. They are disappointed that Buck was not able to finish the test.

1.7) _____ Why is Thornton crying at the end of the story?
- A. Thornton is happy and proud of Buck for passing the test.
- B. Thornton is sad that he has to sell Buck.
- C. Thornton is angry with Buck for not performing his best.
- D. Thornton is sad because he lost money in the bet.

1.8) _____ Why does Buck bite Thornton's hand before and after the challenge?
- A. Buck does not trust Thornton.
- B. Buck is angry and wants to hurt Thornton.
- C. Buck did not want to participate in the challenge.
- D. Buck is showing his love for Thornton.

1.9) What does it mean to be an active reader? _____

_____

_____

_____

Match the words with the descriptions.

1.10) _____ comprehension

1.11) _____ genre

1.12) _____ inference

- A. a category or style of something
- B. the process of understanding a text
- C. a guess or speculation a reader makes based on the evidence given in a text

What is Thoroughness?

If you miss one number or one decimal point in an equation, the answer will be incorrect. If you miscalculated how much money someone owes you, or how much you owe someone else, your carelessness could cost you a lot! Thoroughness is taking care of details in order to do things right. You can practice thoroughness by checking your work, keeping things clean and organized, and finishing the whole project. Details make a difference!

2. THEMES IN LITERARY WORKS

Objectives:

- Analyze, make inferences, and draw conclusions about theme and genre in literary texts.
- Analyze literary works that share similar themes across cultures.
- Analyze how the central characters' qualities influence the theme of a fictional work and resolution of the central conflict.

Vocabulary:

theme – the central message or insight revealed in a work of literature

SO WHAT?

"So what?" is an excellent question to ask when you are thinking about the purpose of a literary work. The **theme** of a piece of literature, poem, movie, or even a video clip on YouTube is the message that the author wants the audience to understand. When deciding on a theme, authors determine what insight or idea they want their audience to remember from reading a work. Theme is a very important element if you are reading or writing. After all, sending or receiving the message is the main reason most people read, write, speak, draw, create a film, or engage in any other activity that has to do with communication.

Learning to find the theme of a literary work aids your comprehension and retention.

Another important part of being an active reader is looking for the central message from the story. However, the theme of a work is sometimes difficult to find because it is rarely stated directly. When looking for the theme of a literary work, ask yourself, "What does the author of this work want me to understand about people or about life?" The theme is often revealed through the characters' actions in the story, the consequences to their actions, the plot, the conflict, the resolution of the conflict, and the tone of the story. Theme is *not* a summary of the story, nor is it expressed as a single word. Instead, we express theme as a statement of a universal truth about people or about life.

Theme is...

- the central message or insight revealed in a literary work.
- a general statement about people or life.
- often expressed indirectly.
- revealed through characters' actions and their consequences, plot, conflict, resolution of conflict, and tone.

Theme is NOT...

- the topic of a work.
- a summary of the plot.
- the conflict.
- the purpose of the work.
- stated as a single word.

Let's practice understanding theme as it relates to poetry. Sometimes, it is easier to find the theme in a poem because poems often state observations about people or life. Also, poems use fewer words than stories; thus, the reader is able to focus on the message presented. Often, poems present the theme through images, or word pictures. Each of the three poems you will read has a different image used to present the theme of the poem.

#1

"The Road Not Taken"
by Robert Frost

Two roads diverged in a yellow wood,
And sorry I could not travel both
And be one traveler, long I stood
And looked down one as far as I could
To where it bent in the undergrowth;

Then took the other, as just as fair,
And having perhaps the better claim,
Because it was grassy and wanted wear;
Though as for that, the passing there
Had worn them really about the same,

And both that morning equally lay
In leaves no step had trodden black.
Oh, I kept the first for another day!
Yet knowing how way leads to way,
I doubted if I should ever come back.

I shall be telling this with a sigh
Somewhere ages and ages hence:
Two roads diverged in a wood, and I—
I took the one less traveled by,
And that has made all the difference.

Poem 352 from *Manyoshu*

by Sami Mansei

Living in this world—
to what shall I compare it?
It's like a boat
rowing out at break of day,
leaving no trace behind.

from *The Rubaiyat*

by Omar Khayyam

The caravan of life shall always pass
Beware that is fresh as sweet young grass
Let's not worry about what tomorrow will amass
Fill my cup again, this night will pass, alas

Now, let's look at each poem more closely and try to determine its theme.

POEM #1
"THE ROAD NOT TAKEN"

The three poems come from three very different cultures. The first one is written by Robert Frost, a man often referred to as "America's poet." "The Road Not Taken" is one of his most famous works. The next poem is from the Japanese culture, and it is from a book of poems called *Manyoshu* (meaning "Collection of Ten Thousand Leaves"), the oldest collection of Japanese poetry. The last poem is written by a man from the Middle East, Omar Khayyam. The poem is from a book called *The Rubaiyat*. Omar Khayyam lived in Persia (now Iran) around the year 1100 AD.

Read these poems again, this time looking for the theme (message) of each poem and the image that is used to present the theme. As you read, try to decide for yourself the message the author wants you to understand. With poetry, there is not usually just one right way to understand it. As long as you support your analysis with evidence from the text, you can determine the message for yourself.

If we take the words of the poem literally (without looking for any underlying meaning), it seems to be about the poet walking on a dirt road in the woods. He comes to a place where the road splits in two and goes in different directions. The roads have not been walked on this morning. They are about the same, but one is a little more used and the other a little less used. The poet wants to go both ways, but he understands that he cannot. He must choose a direction to take, so he decides to take the one that "wanted wear," the one that was "less traveled by." The poet admits that he probably will not return to the road not taken. The speaker says in the last line, "And that has made all the difference." Without the figurative or underlying meaning of the poem, the last line is somewhat confusing.

Now, to understand the figurative meaning and the message of the poem, think about the images the poet uses. In this poem, the main image is the path in the woods that comes to a fork. The speaker must decide which way to go, and he knows he cannot travel on both roads. Ask yourself, "What could the author be trying to communicate through the image of a fork in the road?" Most people understand this poem to be about choices in life. Read the poem again with this idea in mind. The speaker says that the two choices are equal (not one right and one wrong), but that one is more popular than the other. The speaker chooses the less-popular option, and he remarks that the decision he made "has made all the difference."

Remember, to find the theme, ask yourself, "What does the author want me to understand about life?" If the topic of the poem is decisions, then the theme could be expressed this way: The decisions we make have an impact on our lives and often determine the direction and course of our lives. When you choose one path of life, you can't choose the other at the same time, and life rarely allows us go back and remake our choices. Remember, a theme can be expressed many different ways, depending on the reader's interpretation of the poem.

POEM #2
POEM 352 FROM *MANYOSHU*

In this poem, the speaker compares life to a row boat. A row boat that rows out in the morning leaves no mark once the waves have closed in behind it.

Now, look for the deeper meaning behind the image of the row boat. How is life similar to a row boat setting sail? As you think about the image, what ideas occur to you? A row boat is a small boat, powered by the person rowing it. The boat moves as quickly or as slowly as the person rowing, and it moves in the direction that the rower steers it. The row boat sails, "leaving no trace behind," no way to return in the exact way it came. The speaker of the poem tells us the boat represents human life.

After considering the meaning behind the images of the poem, state the theme of the poem in your own words. One example of a statement of theme from this poem is as follows: A person controls the direction his life takes, and once he chooses a certain way, he cannot go back exactly the way he came and choose another direction.

POEM #3
FROM *THE RUBAIYAT*

The poet speaks of a passing caravan. A caravan is a group traveling together, traditionally on camels and other pack animals, along the trade routes carrying goods. He gives the warning to beware of fresh grass and says not to worry about tomorrow because the night is passing.

Looking at the poem on a deeper level, you can see that the journey of the caravan represents life. Remembering that the poet lived in the Middle East will help you to better understand the poem. Why do you think the speaker of the poem says to beware of "sweet young grass"? Perhaps he is telling the reader to beware of being drawn away from the path by something that seems appealing. The speaker also tells the reader not to worry about tomorrow, but to enjoy himself, because the night will soon pass. This advice applies to life as well.

Putting all these ideas together, we can state the theme of the poems as follows: The journey of life is short, so don't allow anything to distract you from your purpose. Live your life to the fullest each day because you only have one life to live, and it will soon be over.

Even though these poems come from three very different cultures and time periods, the ideas presented in the poems are similar. Let's look at some of the unifying elements.

1 – They use images of some kind of a journey to represent life.
  • In "The Road Not Taken" the journey is a hike through the woods.
  • In Poem 352 the journey is a row boat setting sail.
  • In the poem from *The Rubaiyat*, the journey is the path a caravan follows.
2 – The message of each poem relates to the temporary nature of life.
3 – Each poem indicates that we must make choices that determine the course of our lives. In making these choices we often have to give up something to get something else.

After carefully examining the three poems, you can see that they present similar themes; each poem just uses a different image to convey the message to the reader. As you read a literary work, try to look for the message the author wants you to understand.

Take a Hint: Examine, Recall, Apply! When you are answering multiple choice questions, take three steps to help boost success.
  ✔ Step one is to **examine**. In this step you read the question and the possible answers. Really pay attention to what information is being asked for. Look for any information that is given for you to use.
  ✔ Step two is to **recall**. Take a moment to think about the topic of the question. Think about what you already know about this topic. How does the information fit in with what you know?
  ✔ Step three is to **apply**. Read ALL of the possible answers and eliminate any answers that do not apply to the question. Consider the information being asked for and the possible answers you have left. Apply what you know to select the best possible answer to the question being asked.

Read the poem.

"The Men That Don't Fit In"
by Robert Service

There's a race of men that don't fit in,
A race that can't stay still;
So they break the hearts of kith and kin,
And they roam the world at will.
They range the field and they rove the flood,
And they climb the mountain's crest;
Theirs is the curse of the gypsy blood,
And they don't know how to rest.

If they just went straight they might go far;
They are strong and brave and true;
But they're always tired of the things that are,
And they want the strange and new.
They say: "Could I find my proper groove,
What a deep mark I would make!"
So they chop and change, and each
    fresh move
Is only a fresh mistake.

And each forgets, as he strips and runs
With a brilliant, fitful pace,
It's the steady, quiet, plodding ones
Who win in the lifelong race.
And each forgets that his youth has fled,
Forgets that his prime is past,
Till he stands one day, with a hope that's dead,
In the glare of the truth at last.

He has failed, he has failed; he has missed
    his chance;
He has just done things by half.
Life's been a jolly good joke on him,
And now is the time to laugh.
Ha, ha! He is one of the Legion Lost;
He was never meant to win;
He's a rolling stone, and it's bred in the bone;
He's a man who won't fit in.

Choose the correct answers.

2.1) _____ Which word best defines theme?
      A. type   B. message   C. rhyme   D. image

2.2) _____ What is the curse of "the men who don't fit in"?
      A. Like gypsies, they can't stay in one place very long.
      B. They are hopeless.
      C. They are forgetful.
      D. They become tired easily.

2.3) _____ What is the theme of this poem?
- A. Live life to the fullest.
- B. Don't follow the crowd.
- C. When you make your own rules you will succeed.
- D. Constantly becoming bored with the way things are can have consequences.

2.4) _____ How does the poet feel about the men who don't fit in?
- A. He likes them.
- B. He thinks they are failures.
- C. He wants to be like them.
- D. He approves of their ideas.

2.5) _____ What is the meaning of the phrase in the next to last line, "He's a rolling stone"?
- A. He lives in the mountains.
- B. He takes lots of vacations but always goes home.
- C. He likes to stay in one place but studies other places.
- D. He moves around from place to place frequently.

Define the term.

2.6) theme – _____

_____

Check   Correct   Recheck

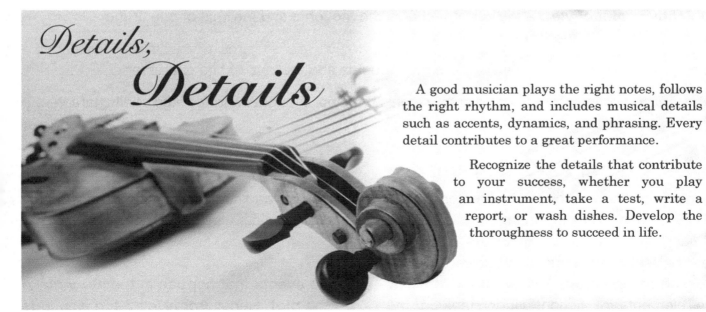

Details, Details

A good musician plays the right notes, follows the right rhythm, and includes musical details such as accents, dynamics, and phrasing. Every detail contributes to a great performance.

Recognize the details that contribute to your success, whether you play an instrument, take a test, write a report, or wash dishes. Develop the thoroughness to succeed in life.

3. ELEMENTS OF FICTION STORIES

Objectives:

- Analyze how the central characters' qualities influence the theme of a fictional work and resolution of the central conflict.
- Understand, make inferences, and draw conclusions about the structure and elements of fiction.
- Analyze plot developments to determine whether and how conflicts are resolved.
- Explain how the values and beliefs of particular characters are affected by the historical and cultural setting of a literary work.
- Analyze different forms of point of view, including limited versus omniscient, and subjective versus objective.

Vocabulary:

characterization – the way the characters are portrayed in a story

conflict – the problem in a story

first-person point of view – the narrator is a character in the story

objective point of view – the narrator tells the story without giving any insight into the thoughts and feelings of the characters

plot – the events that happen in a story

point of view – the perspective from which a story is told

subjective point of view – the narrator shares the thoughts and feelings of one or more characters in the story

third-person limited – the narrator tells the thoughts and feelings of one character

third-person omniscient – the narrator reveals the inner thoughts and feelings of all characters in a story

As you learned in Lesson 1, the main purpose of fiction stories is to entertain the reader. When you understand the elements of fiction and how they affect the story, you can better understand and appreciate the story. Throughout this Lesson, we will review the elements of fiction. Understanding the elements of a fiction story will help you to make inferences and understand the theme of the work more clearly.

PLOT

The events that happen in the story make up the **plot**. Recall from Unit 3 the elements

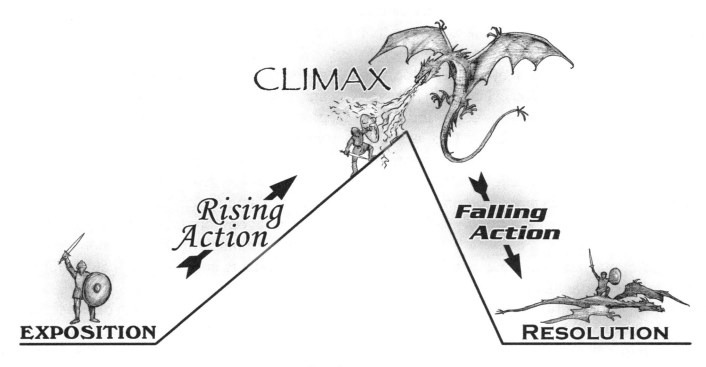

Plot diagram

of plot: exposition, rising action, climax, falling action, and resolution. In order to have a plot, a story must have a **conflict**, or a problem. The plot of the story is shaped by the central conflict.

Let's briefly review the elements of plot. Notice that each element of plot has something to do with the conflict of the story.

- **Exposition** – In the beginning of the story, the characters and setting are described, and the conflict is introduced.
- **Rising Action** – We learn more information about the characters and conflict. The conflict deepens, creating suspense in the story.
- **Climax** – The conflict reaches its peak. The climax is the highest point of action in a story.
- **Falling Action** – We learn the outcome of the climax. The action settles down toward the end of the story.
- **Resolution** – The conflict is resolved. The story ties up any loose ends.

Understanding the plot of a story can help you understand the story's theme or message. When trying to determine the theme, look for the message or truth that the plot reveals about the subject of the story.

CHARACTERIZATION

Looking at the way the characters are portrayed in a story can also help you understand the theme. **Characterization** is one important way that an author presents his or her ideas. The author designs the characters to possess certain qualities, values, and beliefs, and these qualities often determine how the characters act and the consequences of their actions. The characters' actions and their consequences influence the theme of the work. For example, an author who portrays a character who is punished for telling a lie is conveying the message of the importance of telling the truth.

Understanding how central characters change throughout the story is necessary in finding the theme of a story. Often, the central character of a story learns a lesson, and that lesson is related to the theme of the story. In the novel *The Outsiders* by S. E. Hinton, the main character, Ponyboy, learns the lesson that violence does not solve his problems; it actually makes them worse. This lesson is related to the theme that communication and understanding are more effective than violence in solving differences among groups of people.

POINT OF VIEW

In a story, point of view determines how the reader understands the story. The **point of view** of a story is the perspective from which it is told. If a story is told from **first-person point of view**, the reader sees and understands everything the main character sees and understands because the narrator is a character in the story, usually the main character. If the story is told from **third-person point of view**, however, the reader knows only what the narrator reveals.

The narrator in the third-person point of view can be objective or subjective. In the **objective point of view**, the narrator tells the story without giving any insight into the thoughts and feelings of the characters. The third-person objective point of view makes the narrator seem as if he is an onlooker from the outside, only sharing his observations about the events as they happen in the story. In the **subjective point of view**, the narrator shares the thoughts and feelings of one or more characters in the story. If a story is told in **third-person limited** point of view, the narrator tells the thoughts and feelings of one character; if it is told in **third-person omniscient**, the narrator reveals the inner thoughts and feelings of all characters in a story.

All of the elements of fiction discussed in this Lesson—plot, characterization, and point of view—influence the theme. The plot reveals the theme through the events of the story and the resolution of the main conflict. Characterization reveals theme by portraying the characters' qualities, which influence their actions and consequences. The point of view of a story determines how the reader understands the plot and the characters' reactions to the events of the story and allows the reader to understand the message the author wants to convey.

Read the story.

After Twenty Years
by O. Henry

The policeman on the beat moved up the avenue impressively. The impressiveness was habitual and not for show, for spectators were few. The time was barely 10 o'clock

at night, but chilly gusts of wind with a taste of rain in them had well nigh depeopled the streets.

Trying doors as he went, twirling his club with many intricate and artful movements, turning now and then to cast his watchful eye adown the pacific thoroughfare, the officer, with his stalwart **[sturdy]** form and slight swagger, made a fine picture of a guardian of the peace. The vicinity was one that kept early hours. Now and then you might see the lights of a cigar store or of an all-night lunch counter; but the majority of the doors belonged to business places that had long since been closed.

When about midway of a certain block the policeman suddenly slowed his walk. In the doorway of a darkened hardware store a man leaned, with an unlighted cigar in his mouth. As the policeman walked up to him the man spoke up quickly.

"It's all right, officer," he said, reassuringly. "I'm just waiting for a friend. It's an appointment made twenty years ago. Sounds a little funny to you, doesn't it? Well, I'll explain if you'd like to make certain it's all straight. About that long ago there used to be a restaurant where this store stands—'Big Joe' Brady's restaurant."

"Until five years ago," said the policeman. "It was torn down then."

The man in the doorway struck a match and lit his cigar. The light showed a pale, square-jawed face with keen eyes, and a little white scar near his right eyebrow. His scarfpin was a large diamond, oddly set.

"Twenty years ago tonight," said the man, "I dined here at 'Big Joe' Brady's with Jimmy Wells, my best chum, and the finest chap in the world. He and I were raised here in New York, just like two brothers, together. I was eighteen and Jimmy was twenty. The next morning I was to start for the West to make my fortune. You couldn't have dragged Jimmy out of New York; he thought it was the only place on earth. Well, we agreed that night that we would meet here again exactly twenty years from that date and time, no matter what our conditions might be or from what distance we might have to come. We figured that in twenty years each of us ought to have our destiny worked out and our fortunes made, whatever they were going to be."

"It sounds pretty interesting," said the policeman. "Rather a long time between meets, though, it seems to me. Haven't you heard from your friend since you left?"

"Well, yes, for a time we corresponded," said the other. "But after a year or two we lost track of each other. You see, the West is a pretty big proposition, and I kept

hustling around over it pretty lively. But I know Jimmy will meet me here if he's alive, for he always was the truest, staunchest **[most principled or loyal]** old chap in the world. He'll never forget. I came a thousand miles to stand in this door tonight, and it's worth it if my old partner turns up."

The waiting man pulled out a handsome watch, the lids of it set with small diamonds.

"Three minutes to ten," he announced. "It was exactly ten o'clock when we parted here at the restaurant door."

"Did pretty well out West, didn't you?" asked the policeman.

"You bet! I hope Jimmy has done half as well. He was a kind of plodder, though, good fellow as he was. I've had to compete with some of the sharpest wits going to get my pile. A man gets in a groove in New York. It takes the West to put a razor-edge on him."

The policeman twirled his club and took a step or two.

"I'll be on my way. Hope your friend comes around all right. Going to call time on him sharp?"

"I should say not!" said the other. "I'll give him half an hour at least. If Jimmy is alive on earth he'll be here by that time. So long, officer."

"Good-night, sir," said the policeman, passing on along his beat, trying doors as he went.

There was now a fine, cold drizzle falling, and the wind had risen from its uncertain puffs into a steady blow. The few foot passengers astir in that quarter hurried dismally and silently along with coat collars turned high and pocketed hands. And in the door of the hardware store the man who had come a thousand miles to fill an appointment, uncertain almost to absurdity, with the friend of his youth, smoked his cigar and waited.

About twenty minutes he waited, and then a tall man in a long overcoat, with collar turned up to his ears, hurried across from the opposite side of the street. He went directly to the waiting man.

"Is that you, Bob?" he asked, doubtfully.

"Is that you, Jimmy Wells?" cried the man in the door.

"Bless my heart!" exclaimed the new arrival, grasping both the other's hands with his own. "It's Bob, sure as fate. I was certain I'd find you here if you were still in existence. Well, well, well!—twenty years is a long time. The old restaurant's gone, Bob; I wish it had lasted, so we could have had another dinner there. How has the West treated you, old man?"

"Bully; it has given me everything I asked it for. You've changed lots, Jimmy. I never thought you were so tall by two or three inches."

"Oh, I grew a bit after I was twenty."

"Doing well in New York, Jimmy?"

"Moderately. I have a position in one of the city departments. Come on, Bob; we'll go around to a place I know of, and have a good long talk about old times."

The two men started up the street. The man from the West, his egotism enlarged by success, was beginning to outline the history of his career. The other, submerged in his overcoat, listened with interest.

At the corner stood a drug store, brilliant with electric lights. When they came into this glare each of them turned simultaneously to gaze upon the other's face.

The man from the West stopped suddenly and released his arm.

"You're not Jimmy Wells," he snapped. "Twenty years is a long time, but not long enough to change a man's nose from a Roman to a pug."

"It sometimes changes a good man into a bad one," said the tall man. "You've been under arrest for ten minutes, 'Silky' Bob. Chicago thinks you may have dropped over our way and wires us she wants to have a chat with you. Going quietly, are you? That's sensible. Now, before we go on to the station here's a note I was asked to hand you. You may read it here at the window. It's from Patrolman Wells."

The man from the West unfolded the little piece of paper handed him. His hand was steady when he began to read, but it trembled a little by the time he had finished. The note was rather short.

Bob

I was at the appointed place on time. When you struck the match to light your cigar I saw it was the face of the man wanted in Chicago. Somehow I couldn't do it myself, so I went around and got a plainclothesman [a police officer dressed as a civilian] to do the job.

Jimmy

Choose the correct answers.

3.1) _____ Why doesn't Jimmy reveal himself to Bob?

    A. He is ashamed that he hasn't been as successful as Bob.

    B. He is angry at Bob for something that Bob did to him.

    C. He wants to surprise Bob later on.

    D. He discovers who Bob really is and can't bring himself to reveal his identity.

3.2) _____ Why doesn't Jimmy recognize Bob right away as "Silky Bob"?

    A. It is night time, and all the stores are closed, so it is dark outside.

    B. Bob is wearing a disguise so Jimmy won't recognize him.

    C. Bob is wearing a disguise so the police won't recognize his face as the one of a wanted man.

    D. Bob asked a stranger to pretend to be him so that Jimmy wouldn't recognize him.

3.3) _____ After reading the entire story, what can you determine is the main conflict?

    A. Bob is waiting for Jimmy to show up to their designated meeting place.

    B. Once he sees Bob's face, Jimmy does not want to reveal his identity to Bob.

    C. The restaurant where the two men were supposed to meet was torn down.

    D. Bob is afraid that he is going to get caught.

3.4) _____ What is the climax of the story?

    A. The plainclothes police officer confronts Bob and tells Bob that he is under arrest.

    B. Jimmy and Bob discuss Bob's success.

    C. Bob explains to the policeman (Jimmy) why he is waiting outside the restaurant.

    D. Bob reads the note that Jimmy wrote explaining why he didn't reveal his identity to Bob.

3.5) _____ Which statement tells the resolution of the conflict?

    A. The plainclothes police officer confronts Bob and tells Bob that he is under arrest.

    B. Jimmy and Bob discuss Bob's success.

    C. Bob explains to the policeman (Jimmy) why he is waiting outside the restaurant.

    D. Bob reads the note that Jimmy wrote explaining why he didn't reveal his identity to Bob.

3.6) _____ Which of the following statements describes a characteristic of Jimmy?

    A. He is lazy because he is late meeting Bob.

    B. He is honest and fulfills his duty as a police officer.

    C. He is fearful of confronting Bob.

    D. He approves of Bob's behavior.

3.7) _____ What is the point of view, and how does it affect the story?
    A. The point of view is first-person, allowing the reader to understand Bob's thoughts.
    B. The point of view is third-person objective, allowing the reader to see the events and the characters' outward reactions.
    C. The point of view is third-person limited, allowing the reader to understand only Jimmy's inner thoughts.
    D. The point of view is third-person omniscient, allowing the reader to understand all the characters' thoughts and inner feelings.

3.8) _____ Based on the resolution of the conflict and the characters' qualities and actions, what can you infer is the major theme of the story?
    A. Don't make a promise you can't keep.
    B. It is important to do the right thing, even if it is difficult.
    C. You should always check the facts before making a judgment.
    D. Sometimes it is necessary to break a law to help a friend.

Fill in the blanks.

3.9) The perspective from which a story is told is the _____ _____ _____.

Match the types of point of view with the descriptions.

3.10) _____ first-person

3.11) _____ objective

3.12) _____ subjective

3.13) _____ third-person limited

3.14) _____ third-person omniscient

    A. The narrator reveals the thoughts of one or more of the characters.

    B. The narrator is a character in the story.

    C. The narrator reveals the thoughts of only one character.

    D. The narrator reveals the thoughts of all the characters.

    E. The narrator only reveals actions that can be observed.

Describe the elements used in a plot.

3.15) conflict – _____

_____

3.16) exposition – _____

_____

3.17) rising action – _____

_____

3.18) climax – _____

_____

3.19) falling action – _____

_____

3.20) resolution – _____

_____

Check   Correct   Recheck

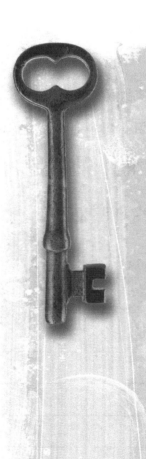

FIVE KEYS TO THOROUGHNESS

1 – Plan Ahead: Think through a project and all the necessary details. What is the goal? When must you finish? What supplies do you need? Does the project involve others? Do others know what is expected of them?

2 – Write It Down: Document your plan so that you know what you are doing. This also makes it easier to share your plan with others. Make a checklist of things to do so that you do not overlook or forget any details.

3 – Pursue Excellence: Quality control is your responsibility. Do not assume others will correct your mistakes or clean up your messes. Take responsibility for your work and do things right.

4 – Double Check: Look over your assignment for correct spelling, punctuation, and grammar. Check your answers before finishing a test. Do not let hastiness cause sloppiness or waste.

5 – Finish the Job: Do not get bogged down in details that do not help you reach the goal. Finish your work instead of getting stuck with unfinished assignments.

(Each answer, 5 points)
Choose the correct answers.

1.01) _____ What is a theme?
    A. the topic of a literary work
    B. the message or insight revealed by a literary work
    C. the plot of a story
    D. the main idea stated as one word

1.02) _____ The perspective from which a story is told is the ___.
    A. point of view   B. plot   C. rising action   D. conflict

1.03) _____ An inference is ___.
    A. an alternate ending to a story
    B. a character trait
    C. a detail revealed in the story
    D. a guess you make based on the details a story gives

1.04) _____ The word that refers to the category or style of a literary work is ___.
    A. inference   B. theme   C. genre   D. topic

Match the plot elements with the descriptions.

1.05) _____ conflict

1.06) _____ exposition

1.07) _____ rising action

1.08) _____ climax

1.09) _____ falling action

1.010) _____ resolution

A. The conflict reaches its peak.

B. the problem in a story

C. The conflict deepens, creating suspense in the story.

D. The characters, setting, and conflict are introduced.

E. The problem is resolved and the story ties up any loose ends.

F. The action settles down toward the end of the story.

Choose the correct answers.

1.011) _____ Which of the following shows how O. Henry uses characterization to display the theme in "After Twenty Years?"
    A. Bob is portrayed as having a "pale, square-jawed face with keen eyes."
    B. Jimmy shows his honesty and sense of duty by turning in a wanted criminal.
    C. Bob says that the man pretending to be Jimmy is taller than he remembered.
    D. Bob has a diamond-studded watch and a diamond scarfpin.

1.012) _____ Which of the following could be a statement of theme in a story?

    A. loyalty

    B. friendship

    C. A policeman turns in a wanted criminal who happens to be an old friend of his.

    D. Even though it can be difficult, it is important to do the right thing.

Read the poem; then choose the correct answers.

---

from *Versos Sencillos* (Simple Verses) XXXIX
by José Martí

I cultivate white roses	And for the brute who tears from me
In January as in July	The heart with which I live,
For the honest friend who freely	I nurture neither grubs nor thistles,
Offers me his hand.	But cultivate white roses.

1.013) _____ The image the poet uses to convey the theme is ___.

    A. white roses   B. January   C. kindness   D. friend

1.014) _____ What is the theme of the poem?

    A. Gardening is an enjoyable activity.

    B. White roses represent kindness.

    C. Treat your friends and your enemies with kindness.

    D. Honesty is the key to a good friendship.

1.015) _____ What do *grubs* and *thistles* most likely represent in this poem?

    A. revenge   B. love   C. enemies   D. kindness

Match the types of point of view with the descriptions.

1.016) _____ first-person

1.017) _____ objective

1.018) _____ subjective

1.019) _____ third-person limited

1.020) _____ third-person omniscient

    A. The narrator reveals the thoughts of only one character.

    B. The narrator only reveals actions that can be observed.

    C. The narrator is a character in the story.

    D. The narrator reveals the thoughts of all characters.

    E. The narrator reveals the thoughts of one or more characters.

Check   Correct   Recheck

4. THE LANGUAGE OF POETRY

Objectives:

- Understand, make inferences, and draw conclusions about the structure and elements of poetry.
- Understand, make inferences, and draw conclusions about how an author's use of sensory language creates imagery in a literary text.
- Explain the effect of figurative language, such as similes and extended metaphors, on a literary text.

Vocabulary:

extended metaphor – a comparison that is developed throughout an entire poem

figurative language – language that is not meant to be taken literally

hyperbole *[hahy-PUR-buh-lee]* – an exaggerated statement often used for the purpose of humor

irony – the literal message of the words, situation, or character is the opposite of what the reader would expect

metaphor *[MET-uh-fawr]* – suggests a comparison between two things without using "like" or "as"

personification *[per-son-uh-fi-KEY-shuhn]* – giving inanimate (nonliving) objects human characteristics

sensory language – words and phrases that appeal to the five senses – sight, hearing, touch, taste, and smell; also called imagery

simile *[SIM-uh-lee]* – uses the words "like" or "as" to show a comparison between two things

symbol – something that represents something else

FIGURATIVE LANGUAGE

What makes poetry different from other types of writing? You have probably noticed that poetry has a certain structure; instead of using paragraphs, the lines are divided into stanzas. You also might say that poetry rhymes, but that characteristic only describes some poems, not all of them. One of the main qualities that makes poetry unique is the language it uses.

Poetry is rich in **figurative language**, language that is not meant to be taken literally. Since poetry uses fewer words to convey a message than prose (ordinary writing) does, the words that a poem uses need to be meaningful. Figurative language allows the writer to create meaning by suggesting a comparison between two things and by deviating from the literal way of expressing an idea.

Simile

A **simile** is a type of figurative language the uses the words "like" or "as" to show a comparison between two things. In the following poem, the speaker uses a simile to compare the woman he loves to a rose and a song.

---

excerpt from "A Red, Red Rose"

by Robert Burns

O, my love's like a red, red rose,
That's newly sprung in June:
O, my love's like the melody,
That's sweetly play'd in tune.

Metaphor

Another type of figurative language used to make comparisons is a metaphor. A **metaphor** suggests a comparison between two things without using "like" or "as." Sometimes, a metaphor will imply a comparison, and other times, a metaphor will state that something *is* something else. Let's look at a couple of examples.

---

excerpt from "Hope"

by Emily Dickinson

Hope is the thing with feathers
That perches in the soul,
And sings the tune—without the words,
And never stops at all.

In the poem "Hope," the speaker compares hope with a bird ("thing with feathers"). The speaker states directly that hope is a bird.

Then next example is one that you have already analyzed for theme. Now, try to find the metaphor.

---

excerpt from *The Rubaiyat*

by Omar Khayyam

The caravan of life shall always pass
Beware that is fresh as sweet young grass
Let's not worry about what tomorrow will amass
Fill my cup again, this night will pass, alas

Did you notice the metaphor in the poem by Omar Khayyam? The speaker suggests the comparison between life and a caravan, implying that life is a journey.

Extended Metaphor

An **extended metaphor** is a comparison that is developed throughout an entire poem. "The Railway Train" by Emily Dickinson makes a comparison throughout the poem. She does not state the comparison directly; instead she describes the train as something else. Try to understand the comparison as you read by picturing the train in your mind as she describes it.

"The Railway Train"

by Emily Dickinson

I like to see it lap the miles,
And lick the valleys up,
And stop to feed itself at tanks;
And then, prodigious, step

Around a pile of mountains,
And, supercilious, peer
In shanties by the sides of roads;
And then a quarry pare

To fit its sides, and crawl between,
Complaining all the while
In horrid, hooting stanza;
Then chase itself down the hill

And neigh like [1]Boanerges;
Then, punctual as a star,
Stop—docile and omnipotent—
At its own stable door.

Did you see the comparison? If not, read the final stanza again. Words like "neigh" and "stable" give us a hint that the speaker is comparing the train to a large horse. Throughout the entire poem, the speaker implies the comparison by describing the train as a horse, giving it horselike actions and movements.

Personification

Another type of figurative language is **personification**, giving inanimate (nonliving) objects human characteristics. Personification allows the poet to creatively describe something that is not human as if it were a person. Let's look at another poem by Emily Dickinson to demonstrate personification.

"The Sky Is Low"

by Emily Dickinson

The sky is low, the clouds are mean,
A traveling flake of snow
Across a barn or through a rut
Debates if it will go.

A narrow wind complains all day
How someone treated him;
Nature, like us, is sometimes caught
Without her diadem. **[crown]**

---

[1]*Boanerges* means "sons of thunder."

This poem gives human qualities to elements of nature. What human qualities do you see in this poem? In the first line, the speaker describes the clouds as "mean," and at the end of the first stanza, the speaker says that the snowflake "debates" where it is going to travel. In the second stanza, the speaker gives the wind the action of complaining. At the end of the poem, the speaker summarizes by saying, "Nature, like us, is sometimes caught / Without her diadem," indicating that nature does not always behave properly and majestically, just as humans do not always act like they should.

Hyperbole

A **hyperbole** is an exaggerated statement often used for the purpose of humor. Many people use hyperboles in their everyday speech, such as in the sentence, "I've told you a million times to clean your room!" Sometimes, a hyperbole is used to have a dramatic effect, as in the next poem.

excerpt from "Concord Hymn"

by Ralph Waldo Emerson

By the rude bridge that arched the flood,
Their flag to April's breeze unfurled,
Here once the embattled farmers stood,
And fired the shot heard round the world.

The last phrase of the poem demonstrates hyperbole—"the shot heard round the world." The exaggeration in this statement is for dramatic effect.

Irony

Irony occurs when the literal message of the words, situation, or character is the opposite of what the reader would expect. Verbal irony, also called sarcasm, occurs when the literal meaning of someone's words is opposite of the intended meaning. For example, if a student makes the remark, "I can't wait to start on my four hours of homework tonight," you know that the speaker is using verbal irony. Situational irony occurs when a situation turns out differently than how you would expect.

Irony is prevalent in stories as well as poetry. Irony is used to strengthen a message and get the reader thinking. "The Rime of the Ancient Mariner" by Samuel Taylor Coleridge is a very well-known poem. A famous saying that demonstrates irony comes from a stanza of this poem.

excerpt from "Rime of the Ancient Mariner"

by Samuel Taylor Coleridge

Water, water, everywhere,
And all the boards did shrink;
Water, water, everywhere,
Nor any drop to drink.

In the poem, a merchant ship has been blown off course in a storm and has ended up in the Antarctic. The ship is surrounded by ice, and the crew is freezing to death. An albatross (large sea bird) flies to the ship, and the ice breaks up. The wind starts to blow them northward to warmer waters. The bird follows them, but the ancient mariner shoots and kills the bird. Now, the mariner and all the other sailors on the ship are cursed. The ship is now in uncharted waters. In the stanza you just read, it is ironic that the sailors are surrounded by water, yet they are dying of thirst.

Symbolism

In "The Rime of the Ancient Mariner," the albatross is a symbol of hope and hospitality.

A **symbol** is something that represents something else. The albatross was seen as a symbol of good luck by sailors of long ago, and the mariner was wrong to shoot it.

Look at the following stanzas from part one of the same poem narrating the arrival of the albatross. Notice how the sailors praise the albatross as a symbol of hope.

The ice was here, the ice was there,
The ice was all around:
It cracked and growled, and roared and howled,
Like noises in a swound!

At length did cross an Albatross,
Thorough the fog it came;
As it had been a Christian soul,
We hailed it in God's name.

It ate the food it ne'er had eat,
And round and round it flew.
The ice did split with a thunder-fit;
The helmsman steered us through!

And a good south wind sprung up behind;
The Albatross did follow,
And every day, for food or play,
Came to the mariner's hollo!

SENSORY LANGUAGE

In addition to figurative language, sensory language is also widely used in poetry. **Sensory language**, also called imagery, includes words and phrases that appeal to the five senses—sight, hearing, touch, taste, and smell. The purpose of using imagery in a poem is to create a picture in the reader's mind that will help the reader better understand and relate to the poem. Sensory language makes a literary work come alive in the reader's mind by showing a vivid description rather than simply telling about it. Imagery can be found in almost every poem you read. It is one of the strongest language tools a writer uses.

The following poem demonstrates imagery as well as several types of figurative language. As you read, look for words and phrases that help create an image in your mind.

"Autumn Leaves"
by Angelina Wray

In the hush and the lonely silence
Of the chill October night,
Some wizard has worked his magic
With fairy fingers light.

The leaves of the sturdy oak trees
Are splendid with crimson and red.

And the golden flags of the maple
Are fluttering overhead.

Through the tangle of faded grasses
There are trailing vines ablaze,
And the glory of warmth and color
Gleams through the autumn haze.

Like banners of marching armies
That farther and farther go;
Down the winding roads and valleys
The boughs of the sumacs glow.

So open your eyes, little children,
And open your hearts as well,
Till the charm of the bright October
Shall fold you in its spell.

_____

What examples of imagery did you find in this poem? You should have noticed examples of sound, touch, and sight imagery. Look at the table for examples.

Imagery Examples	
Sound	"hush," "silence"
Touch	"chill," "warmth"
Sight	"sturdy oak trees," "crimson and red," "golden flags," "fluttering overhead," "faded grasses," "trailing vines ablaze," "gleams through the autumn haze," "banners of marching armies," "winding roads and valleys"

The imagery in this poem creates a certain effect. It allows the reader to picture the sights of autumn in his or her mind. The poem creates a mood of reflection and solitude through the imagery it uses.

Review

Match the words with the descriptions or examples.

4.1) _____ figurative language

4.2) _____ metaphor

4.3) _____ simile

4.4) _____ hyperbole

4.5) _____ personification

4.6) _____ irony

4.7) _____ symbol

4.8) _____ sensory language

4.9) _____ extended metaphor

A. Tom runs faster than a speeding bullet.

B. The waves high-fived the sand, clapping against the shore.

C. an object that stands for something else, such as a dove standing for peace

D. words and phrases that are not meant to be taken literally

E. Mark's a bear before he has his morning cup of coffee.

F. The literal meaning of a phrase is opposite of its intended meaning.

G. descriptions that give the reader a mental picture

H. a comparison that is developed throughout an entire poem

I. Elena is as busy as a bee.

Read the poem.

excerpt from "Daffodils"

by William Wordsworth

I wandered lonely as a cloud
That floats on high o'er vales and hills,
When all at once I saw a crowd,
A host, of golden daffodils;
Beside the lake, beneath the trees,
Fluttering and dancing in the breeze.

Continuous as the stars that shine
And twinkle on the milky way,
They stretched in never-ending line
Along the margin of a bay;
Ten thousand saw I at a glance,
Tossing their heads in sprightly dance.

Write the correct answers.

4.10) _____ Which phrase from the poem contains a simile?
       A. Ten thousand saw I at a glance
       B. A host, of golden daffodils
       C. Fluttering and dancing in the breeze
       D. I wandered lonely as a cloud that floats on high o'er vales and hills

4.11) _____ Which line contains a hyperbole?
       A. They stretched in never-ending line   C. Beside the lake, beneath the trees
       B. A host, of golden daffodils   D. Tossing their heads in sprightly dance

4.12) _____ Which line contains personification?
       A. Continuous as the stars that shine   C. Fluttering and dancing in the breeze
       B. Beside the lake, beneath the trees   D. And twinkle on the milky way

Write five phrases from the poem that contain visual imagery. (Remember that a phrase is more than one word.)

4.13) _____

4.14) _____

4.15) _____

4.16) _____

4.17) _____

Check   **Correct**   **Recheck**

5. THE SOUND OF POETRY

Objective:

- Understand, make inferences, and draw conclusions about the structure and elements of poetry.

Vocabulary:

alliteration *[uh-lit-uh-REY-shuhn]* – the repetition of beginning sounds in words that are close to each other

meter – the pattern of stressed and unstressed syllables in a poem

onomatopoeia *[on-uh-mat-uh-PEE-uh]* – the use of words to imitate sounds, such as *buzz*, *hiss*, *boom*, and *pop*

rhyme – the repetition of accented vowel sounds at the ends of words

rhyme scheme – the pattern of rhyming words in a poem

rhythm – a musical quality created by stressed and unstressed syllables in spoken words

DEVICES

Just as poetry uses a certain type of language, poetry also has a distinct sound. Most people, when they think of poetry, associate it with rhyming words; however, poetry uses other sound devices as well. We will talk about the sound of poetry in this Lesson.

Alliteration

One common sound device in poetry is **alliteration**, the repetition of beginning sounds in words that are close to each other. Alliteration creates a certain effect in a poem. For example, the repetition of hard consonant sounds, like *k*, can create a rough, harsh sound. On the other hand, the repetition of soft consonant sounds, like *s*, can create a soft, soothing sound.

Notice the alliteration in the following poem.

excerpt from "The Bells"

by Edgar Allen Poe

Hear the loud alarum bells—
Brazen bells!
What a tale of terror, now, their turbulency tells!

The sounds repeated are the *b* sound ("bells—Brazen bells") and the *t* sound ("tale . . . terror . . . turbulency tells"). What kind of mood or sound does the repetition of these consonants create?

Onomatopoeia

Onomatopoeia is another common device used in poetry to create sound. **Onomatopoeia** is the use of words to imitate sounds, such as *buzz, hiss, boom,* and *pop.* Words that use onomatopoeia appeal to the sense of hearing because they provide a specific sound for the reader.

Let's look at another stanza of "The Bells" by Edgar Allen Poe. Find examples of onomatopoeia throughout the first stanza of this poem.

Hear the sledges with the bells—
Silver bells!
What a world of merriment their melody foretells!
How they tinkle, tinkle, tinkle,
In the icy air of night!
While the stars that oversprinkle
All the heavens seem to twinkle
With a crystalline delight;
Keeping time, time, time,
In a sort of Runic rhyme,
To the tintinnabulation that so musically wells
From the bells, bells, bells, bells,
Bells, bells, bells—
From the jingling and the tinkling of the bells.

Which words in this poem use onomatopoeia? Words such as "tinkle" and "jingling" give the reader the sound that the bells are making. This poem also uses repetition to create a certain sound and rhythmic effect.

RHYME AND RHYME SCHEME

Often, poetry contains words that rhyme arranged in a particular pattern. **Rhyme** is created by the repetition of accented vowel sounds at the ends of words, as in *hour* and *flower.* Rhyme is fairly easy to recognize in poetry if you read the poem out loud.

The **rhyme scheme** of a poem is the pattern of rhyming words at the ends of lines. When you determine the rhyme scheme of a poem, look at the last word in each line. Starting with the letter **A**, assign rhyming words the same letter. Start over with each new stanza. Look at the following example

---

excerpt from
"It Is Not Always May"

by Henry Wadsworth Longfellow

The sun is bright,—the air is **clear**,	**A**
The darting swallows soar and **sing**.	**B**
And from the stately elms I **hear**	**A**
The bluebird prophesying **Spring**.	**B**
So blue you winding river **flows**,	**C**
It seems an outlet from the **sky**,	**D**
Where waiting till the west-wind **blows**,	**C**
The freighted clouds at anchor **lie**.	**D**

Since both stanzas follow the same pattern, we would say the poem has an **ABAB** rhyme scheme. Notice that, within a stanza, all ending words that rhyme are given the same letter.

Often, poems contain internal rhyme, which occurs within lines. Look at the following stanza and notice the rhyming words that are placed in the middle of the lines.

excerpt from "The Raven"

by Edgar Allan Poe

Once upon a midnight **dreary**, while I pondered
weak and **weary**,
Over many a quaint and curious volume of
forgotten lore,
While I nodded, nearly **napping**, suddenly there
came a **tapping**,
As of someone gently **rapping**, **rapping** at my
chamber door.
"'Tis some visitor," I muttered, "**tapping** at my
chamber door—
Only this, and nothing more."

RHYTHM AND METER

Rhythm is a musical quality created by stressed and unstressed syllables in spoken words. The best way to understand rhythm is to say a poem aloud so that you can hear the stressed syllables. Read the following stanza out loud and listen to the syllables that you naturally stress.

excerpt from "Rime of the Ancient Mariner"

by Samuel Taylor Coleridge

Water, water, everywhere,
And all the boards did shrink;
Water, water, everywhere,
Nor any drop to drink.

When you read the poem aloud, you probably stress the first syllable in "water" and the first and third syllables in "everywhere." Look at the stanza again; this time, the accented syllables are marked with the symbol ('), and unstressed syllables are marked with the symbol (˘). Notice that the stress marks are placed over the vowels in each syllable.

Wátĕr, wátĕr, éverўwhére,
Ănd áll thĕ bóards dĭd shrínk;
Wátĕr, wátĕr, éverўwhére,
Nŏr ánў dróp tŏ drínk.

The first and third lines have four stressed syllables, and the second and fourth lines have three stressed syllables. This pattern of stressed syllables in a poem is called **meter**. Meter is what gives a poem its musical, rhythmic quality.

As you can see, the devices of alliteration, onomatopoeia, rhyme, and rhythm give poetry its own unique sound. In the next Lesson, you will learn about different forms of poetry that use different patterns of rhyme and meter to create a specific sound.

Match the words with the descriptions.

5.1) _____ rhyme

5.2) _____ rhythm

5.3) _____ meter

5.4) _____ rhyme scheme

5.5) _____ alliteration

5.6) _____ onomatopoeia

A. repeated sounds at the beginning of words

B. a musical quality created by stressed and unstressed syllables in spoken words

C. the repetition of accented vowel sounds at the ends of words

D. words that imitate sounds

E. the rhythmical pattern of stressed and unstressed syllables in a poem

F. the pattern of rhyming words in a poem

Read the poem; then write the correct answers.

excerpt from "Rain in Summer"

by Henry Wadsworth Longfellow

How beautiful is the rain!
After the dust and heat,
In the broad and fiery street,
In the narrow lane,

How beautiful is the rain!
How it clatters along the roofs,
Like the tramp of hoofs
How it gushes and struggles out
From the throat of the overflowing spout!

5.7) What is the rhyme scheme of the first stanza? _____

5.8) What is the rhyme scheme of the second stanza? _____

5.9) Write three examples of onomatopoeia from these two stanzas.

a. _____

b. _____

c. _____

Read the poem; then choose the correct answers.

---

excerpt from "The Raven"

by Edgar Allen Poe

Once upon a midnight dreary, while I pondered weak and weary,
Over many a quaint and curious volume of forgotten lore,
While I nodded, nearly napping, suddenly there came a tapping,
As of someone gently rapping, rapping at my chamber door.
"'Tis some visitor," I muttered, "tapping at my chamber door—
Only this, and nothing more."

5.10) _____ The rhyme scheme of this stanza of the poem is ___.
     A. AABBAA
     B. ABCBBB
     C. ABCABC
     D. ABCDCC

5.11) _____ Each line, except the last one, contains ___ accented syllables.
     A. 8
     B. 10
     C. 6
     D. 4

5.12) _____ The words *while*, *weak*, and *weary* create ___ in the poem.
     A. onomatopoeia
     B. rhyme
     C. rhythm
     D. alliteration

Check   **Correct**   **Recheck**

QUIZ 2

(Each answer, 5 points)
Read the poem; then choose the correct answers.

"Snowy Mountains"
by John Gould Fletcher

Higher and still more high,
Palaces made for cloud,
Above the dingy city-roofs
Blue-white like angels with broad wings,
Pillars of the sky at rest
The mountains from the great plateau
Uprise.

But the world heeds them not;
They have been here now for too long a time.
The world makes war on them,
Tunnels their granite cliffs,
Splits down their shining sides,
Plasters their cliffs with soap-advertisements,
Destroys the lonely fragments of their peace.

Vaster and still more vast,
Peak after peak, pile after pile,
Wilderness still untamed,
To which the future is as was the past,
Barrier spread by Gods,
Sunning their shining foreheads,
Barrier broken down by those who do not need
The joy of time-resisting storm-worn stone,
The mountains swing along
The south horizon of the sky;
Welcoming with wide floors of blue-green ice
The mists that dance and drive before the sun.

2.01) _____ Which statement contains visual imagery?
    A. dingy city-roofs
    B. the world heeds them not
    C. To which the future is as was the past
    D. They have been here now for too long a time

2.02) _____ Which statement contains a metaphor?
  A. Higher and still more high
  B. The mountains from the great plateau
  C. Pillars of the sky at rest
  D. Splits down their shining sides

2.03) _____ Which statement contains a simile?
  A. Barrier spread by Gods
  B. The joy of time-resisting storm-worn stone
  C. The mountains swing along
  D. Blue-white like angels with broad wings

2.04) _____ Which statement contains personification?
  A. Pillars of the sky at rest
  B. The world makes war on them
  C. To which the future is as was the past
  D. The south horizon of the sky.

2.05) _____ *Sunning their shining foreheads* is an example of ___.
  A. simile and rhyme
  B. alliteration and personification
  C. onomatopoeia and personification
  D. rhyme and alliteration

2.06) _____ *The mists that dance and drive before the sun* is an example of ___.
  A. personification
  B. simile
  C. rhyme
  D. hyperbole

2.07) _____ *Palaces made for cloud* is a metaphor describing ___.
  A. the world
  B. another planet
  C. the mountains
  D. the city-roofs

2.08) _____ What is the effect of the imagery used to describe the mountains?
  A. It makes the mountains seem unimportant.
  B. It makes the mountains seem majestic and royal.
  C. It makes the mountains seem dangerous.
  D. It makes the mountains seem appreciated.

2.09) _____ What is the effect of the imagery used to describe the world?
  A. It makes the world seem uncaring and mean toward the mountains.
  B. It makes the world seem appreciative of the mountains.
  C. It makes the world seem loving toward the mountains.
  D. It makes the world seem afraid of the mountains.

Match the words with the descriptions or examples.

2.010) _____ rhythm

2.011) _____ onomatopoeia

2.012) _____ meter

2.013) _____ symbol

2.014) _____ irony

2.015) _____ hyperbole

2.016) _____ extended metaphor

2.017) _____ figurative language

2.018) _____ alliteration

A. "the shot heard round the world"

B. buzz, thump, pop, bam, bang

C. a comparison that is developed throughout an entire poem

D. something that stands for something else

E. words and phrases that are not meant to be taken literally

F. "Water, water, everywhere, / Nor any drop to drink."

G. the rhythmical pattern of stressed and unstressed syllables in a poem

H. a musical quality created by stressed and unstressed syllables

I. repetition of beginning sounds in words that are close together

Read the poem; then choose the correct answers.

"The Arrow and the Song"

by Henry Wadsworth Longfellow

I shot an arrow into the air,
It fell to earth, I knew not where;
For, so swiftly it flew, the sight
Could not follow it in its flight.

I breathed a song into the air,
It fell to earth, I knew not where;
For who has sight so keen and strong
That it can follow the flight of song?

Long, long afterward, in an oak
I found the arrow, still unbroke;
And the song, from beginning to end,
I found again in the heart of a friend.

2.019) _____ What is the rhyme scheme of this poem?
A. AABB
B. ABAB
C. ABCB
D. ABCD

2.020) _____ The line, "That it can follow the flight of song," uses a(n) ___ to compare the arrow and the song.
A. onomatopoeia
B. simile
C. metaphor
D. hyperbole

Check **Correct** **Recheck**

TATTLE-TALE

Details make the difference between "tattling" and reporting facts. Before you tell on another student, ask yourself if you are truly responsible to say anything. Avoid meddling in situations that do not concern you.

If someone annoys you, bumps your chair, or makes faces at you, ignore his or her foolish behavior. If the problem continues, ask the individual to stop disturbing you or ask the teacher if you can sit somewhere else.

If a student threatens or abuses you or others, go directly to a teacher or someone else you can trust. Recognize what happens around you so that you can discern the proper response and give a thorough account to the appropriate authorities.

6. STYLES OF POETRY

Objectives:
- Compare and contrast the purposes and characteristics of different poetic forms.
- Write poems using poetic techniques, figurative language, and graphic elements.

Vocabulary:

couplet – two-line section of a poem

diamante [dee-uh-mahn-TEY] – a seven-line poem composed of words that form the shape of a diamond

epic poem – a long narrative poem that tells about an exaggerated hero who embarks on a quest to achieve something of great or noble worth

free verse – a poem that does not have a rhyme scheme or meter; tries to capture the essence of ordinary speech

haiku [HAHY-koo] – a form of Japanese poetry that has three lines and a specific pattern of syllables

iambic [ahy-AM-bik] **pentameter** – each line of a poem consists of five iambs, each containing one accented syllable

limerick [LIM-er-ik] – a humorous, five-line poem that has a specific rhyme scheme and meter

lyric poem – does not tell a story; rather, it expresses the thoughts and feelings of the speaker of the poem

narrative poem – a poem that tells a story

ode – a lyric poem written to praise or dedicate a person or place

quatrain [KWO-treyn] – four-line section of a poem

sonnet – a poem that has fourteen lines and a specific rhyme scheme and rhythmical pattern

Now that you have learned what kind of language and sound poetry uses, you will learn about the different types of poems and the forms poetry can take. Pay attention as you read about the different types; you will demonstrate these types in your own writing.

Poetry can be about almost anything. A poem can be used to tell a story, to make someone laugh, to express one's feelings, or to describe a person or place. Poems can be serious or funny, lighthearted, or reflective. As you start writing your own poetry, remember, there is not one right way to craft a poem. Poetry writing is both a skill and an art; it allows you to express your creativity and sharpen your talents as a writer.

NARRATIVE

One major style of poetry is the narrative poem. In the last Unit, you learned the definition of a narrative. Simply stated, a narrative is a story. So, a **narrative poem** is a poem that tells a story. Just like a short story, a narrative poem has characters, setting, conflict, and plot. It is usually longer than other styles of poetry. A narrative poem can rhyme, but it does not have to.

An example of a narrative poem is "The Rime of the Ancient Mariner," a poem we discussed earlier in this Unit. This poem has all the elements of a short story—characters, setting, conflict, and plot.

EPIC

An **epic poem** is a long narrative poem that tells about an exaggerated hero who embarks on a quest to achieve something of great or noble worth. The hero of an epic represents the ideals of the culture or society in which he lives. Some famous examples of epics include Homer's *Odyssey* and the Old English epic poem *Beowulf*.

LYRIC

In contrast with a narrative poem, a **lyric poem** does not tell a story; rather, it expresses the thoughts and feelings of the speaker of the poem. Poems that express the speaker's emotions about a single topic are lyric poems. One common type of lyric poem is an **ode**, a lyric poem written to praise or dedicate a person or place.

Look at the following lyric poem—"Upstream" by Carl Sandburg. Think about the following questions as you read: What emotions are expressed in the poem? Who are the men the speaker praises in the poem?

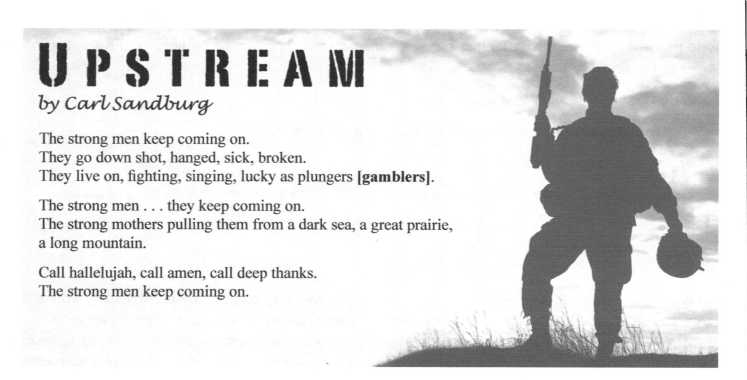

UPSTREAM
by Carl Sandburg

The strong men keep coming on.
They go down shot, hanged, sick, broken.
They live on, fighting, singing, lucky as plungers [**gamblers**].

The strong men . . . they keep coming on.
The strong mothers pulling them from a dark sea, a great prairie,
a long mountain.

Call hallelujah, call amen, call deep thanks.
The strong men keep coming on.

Answer the questions.

6.1) Who are the "strong men" in the poem? _____

_____

6.2) Why does the speaker praise these men? _____

_____

_____

6.3) Why do you think the poem is titled "Upstream"? _____

_____

_____

_____

STRUCTURES OF POETIC FORMS

Narrative and lyric are categories of poems that refer to the content of the poems themselves. We will now look at the structure of poems. Poems can be written in many different forms. Some poems have a specific pattern of rhyme and meter, while others do not.

Free Verse

Poems written in **free verse** do not have a rhyme scheme or meter. Instead, free verse tries to capture the essence and sound of ordinary speech. When you read a free verse poem out loud, it does not usually sound like poetry because it does not have a rhyming or rhythmical pattern. So what makes free verse poetry different from ordinary prose writing? Free verse poetry uses the language of poetry —figurative language and imagery. It also often uses the sound devices of alliteration and onomatopoeia.

The poem that you just read is an example of free verse poetry. Read through the poem once more.

"Upstream"

by Carl Sandburg

The strong men keep coming on.
They go down shot, hanged, sick, broken.
They live on, fighting, singing, lucky as plungers.

The strong men ... they keep coming on.
The strong mothers pulling them from a dark sea,
a great prairie, a long mountain.

Call hallelujah, call amen, call deep thanks.
The strong men keep coming on.

Notice that the poem does not have a rhyme scheme or a rhythmical pattern. It does, however, use sensory language ("dark sea, a great prairie, a long mountain"), figurative language ("lucky as plungers"), repetition ("the strong men,"), and alliteration ("shot . . . sick . . . singing").

Diamante

A simple form of poetry to write and recognize is the diamante. A **diamante** is a seven-line poem composed of words that form the shape of a diamond. It does not have a rhyme scheme or rhythmical pattern; instead, each line is composed of specific word types. Usually, diamantes are poems that link two opposite or distinctly different words together. Look at the **Fig. 6.1**.

How is a diamante written? Notice that **lines one and seven** are one-word antonyms. They are the nouns that are the subject of the poem. **Lines two and six** are made up of two adjectives each that describe the nouns in lines

City
Crowded, Noisy
Going, Running, Bustling
Never sleeps, Awakens early
Working, Walking, Waiting
Quiet, Peaceful
Country

Fig. 6.1

one and seven. **Lines three and five** are made up of three words each ending in -*ing* that tell an action that describes the nouns in lines one and seven. **Line four**, the middle of the poem, is the link between the two words. It contains two words that describe line one and two words that describe line seven. Line four can also be a phrase that shows the comparison between lines one and seven.

(noun 1)

(two adjectives describing noun 1)

(three actions ending in -*ing* describing noun 1)

(two words that relate to noun 1, two words that relate to noun 2)

(three actions ending in -*ing* describing noun 2)

(two adjectives describing noun 2)

(noun 2—antonym)

Morning
Bright, Energetic
Awakening, Rising, Shining
Sun wakes, Sun sleeps
Dwindling, Darkening, Resting
Dark, Peaceful
Evening

Fig. 6.2 Pattern for a diamante

Create your own diamante poem.

6.4)

 **Teacher Check**

Limerick

You have learned about two structures of poetry so far—the narrative, which has no rhyme scheme or meter, and the diamante, which has a specific structure, but no rhyme scheme or meter. Now, we will focus on a poetic form that does have a rhyme scheme and rhythmical pattern—the limerick. A **limerick** is a humorous, five-line poem that has a specific rhyme scheme and meter. The rhyme scheme for a limerick is AABBA, meaning that the first, second, and fifth lines rhyme, and the third and fourth lines rhyme.

Look at the following example of a limerick by Edward Lear, who is known for his humorous poetry. Notice the AABBA rhyme scheme.

There was an Old Man with a **beard**,   A
Who said, "It is just as I **feared**!—   A
Two Owls and a **Hen**,   B
Four Larks and a **Wren**,   B
Have all built their nests in my **beard**!"   A

The meter, or rhythmical pattern, of a limerick is also very specific. The first, second, and fifth lines all have three accented syllables, while the third and fourth lines have two accented syllables. Look at the poem again, this time noticing the meter. The accented syllables are marked with the symbol ('), and unstressed syllables are marked with the symbol (˘). Tap out the rhythm as you read it to yourself.

Thĕre **wás** ăn Ŏld **Mán** wĭth ă **béard**,   3 (accented syllables)

Whŏ **sáid**, "Ĭt ĭs **júst** ăs Ĭ **féared**!   3
Twŏ **Ówls** ănd ă **Hén**,   2
Fŏur **Lárks** ănd ă **Wrén**,   2
Hăve **áll** bŭilt thĕir **nésts** ĭn mў **béard**!" 3

Now, create your own humorous limerick. Make sure that you use the correct rhyme scheme and rhythmical pattern. Many limericks begin with "There was a . . ." because it fits well with the rhythm.

6.5) _____ **(A)**

_____ **(A)**

_____ **(B)**

_____ **(B)**

_____ **(A)**

Haiku

A **haiku** is a form of Japanese poetry that has three lines and a specific pattern of syllables. A haiku does not have a rhyme scheme. Haikus are traditionally written about nature, but you can use the form of a haiku to write about anything. In a haiku, the first and third lines have five syllables each, and the second line has seven syllables. Look at the following examples. Notice that in each poem, the first and third lines have five syllables, and the second line has seven syllables.

Traditional Haiku
by Issa

A giant firefly:
that way, this way, this—
and it passes by.

Modern Haiku
by F. Flath

In my lunch box waits
scrumptious special home-baked treat—
chocolate chip cookie

Now, write your own haiku. You can write about a traditional subject or a more modern one. If you are struggling to come up with something to write, look around you. Write about an ordinary object that you see every day, but describe it with as much sensory and figurative language as you can. Choose only the most descriptive, interesting, precise words to include in your haiku. It is a good idea to leave out any articles (*a, an, the*), unless they are absolutely necessary to your haiku.

Create your own haiku.

6.6) _____

_____

_____

Teacher Check

Sonnet

A sonnet is more complicated than a haiku, limerick, or diamante. A **sonnet** is a poem that has fourteen lines and a specific rhyme scheme and rhythmical pattern. Because of the complex structure, sonnets are difficult to write. Let's look at a sonnet by William Shakespeare, the most well-known sonnet writer (He wrote 154 of them—that we know of!). First, notice the rhyme scheme. Remember, Shakespeare wrote during the 1500s and 1600s, so some of the words' pronunciations have changed since then.

Notice that a sonnet is composed of three four-line sections (called **quatrains**) and one two-line section (called a **couplet**) for a total of fourteen lines. The rhyme scheme of a sonnet is ABAB CDCD EFEF GG.

The content of a sonnet is supported by the structure. The sonnet is divided into two distinct sections—lines 1–8 and lines 9–14.

William Shakespeare

Lines 1–8 introduce the topic of the sonnet. Lines 9–14 show a twist or a change in the focus of the sonnet.

Sonnet XVIII
by William Shakespeare

Shall I compare thee to a summer's **day**?	**A**
Thou art more lovely and more temper**ate**:	**B**
Rough winds do shake the darling buds of **May**,	**A**
And summer's lease hath all too short a **date**:	**B**
Sometime too hot the eye of heaven **shines**,	**C**
And often is his gold complexion **dimm'd**,	**D**
And every fair from fair sometime de**clines**,	**C**
By chance, or nature's changing course un**trimm'd**:	**D**
But thy eternal summer shall not **fade**,	**E**
Nor lose possession of that fair thou **ow'st**,	**F**
Nor shall death brag thou wander'st in his **shade**,	**E**
When in eternal lines to time thou **grow'st**,	**F**
So long as men can breathe, or eyes can **see**,	**G**
So long lives this, and this gives life to **thee**.	**G**

6.7) Read lines 1–8. What is the topic of the first half of the sonnet? _____

_____

_____

_____

6.8) Now, read lines 9–14. Explain how the focus of the sonnet changes in this section. _____

_____

_____

_____

Check   Correct   Recheck

Look at the answers you just wrote. Your first answer should reflect that the first eight lines of the poem deal with the topic of nature, specifically the temporary aspect of beauty and the seasons.

The second half of the poem changes its focus. In lines 9–14, the speaker talks about the woman he loves and says that her beauty is permanent ("But thy eternal summer shall not fade"). The first eight lines of the sonnet present the topic of the sonnet, and the last six lines shift focus to present a truth or insight about the theme.

The last element is the rhythmical pattern, the sonnet's meter. Sonnets are written in **iambic pentameter**—each line has ten syllables, five of which are accented. The pattern of iambic pentameter is soft-HARD / soft-HARD / soft-HARD /soft-HARD / soft-HARD. Let's look at the first line of the poem, this time with the syllables marked.

Shăll Í / cŏmpáre/ thĕe tó / ă súm / mĕr's dáy?

The *penta-* in iambic pentameter means "five," so there are five accented syllables in a line. An *iamb*, also called a foot, is a group of two syllables. In iambic pentameter, a line is separated into five iambs of two syllables, each iamb (group) having one unstressed and one stressed syllable.

Don't worry if iambic pentameter still seems a little confusing. You will learn more about it (and other types of meters) in upper-level English courses.

POETRY WRITING

In this last section, you will be writing your own poem, choosing a style that works best for you. **Table 6.1** shows the guidelines to follow when writing your poem:

TABLE 6.1
❑ Your poem must be at least *twelve* lines long.
❑ Choose an appropriate topic for your poem. Your poem can be narrative or lyric. The subject can be humorous or serious.
❑ It should have a specific form—even if that form is free verse. Your poem can have a rhyme scheme, but it does not have to. If you choose to write a haiku or limerick, you will have to write more than one so that you meet the requirement of twelve lines.
❑ Use figurative language (simile, metaphor, personification, etc.) and sensory language (imagery) in your poem. The words you choose need to be specific and precise. Focus on finding exactly the right words to describe your topic.
❑ Follow the steps of the writing process: plan, draft, revise, proofread and edit, and publish.

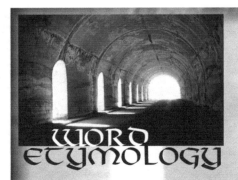

WORD ETYMOLOGY

About 1000 AD, the adjective *thuruh* meant "from side to side; from end to end." The modern derivatives *door* and *thorough* actually come from the same linguistic root referring to a passage or a hole. Thus, thoroughness carried the idea of passing completely through.

Thor•ough•ness *n.* 1: the quality of completeness; 2: not overlooking important details; 3: exhaustive in fulfilling a task

6.9) **PLAN**—Use this area to plan your poem. Choose a topic and brainstorm. Draw a graphic organizer to help generate and organize your ideas.

Topic of Poem: _____

Brainstorming and Organizing

6.10) **DRAFT**—Write a rough draft of your poem. When you are finished drafting, read through your poem and revise it for content and style. Then, proofread and edit your poem.

Title: _____

6.11) PUBLISH—Write a neat, polished final draft of your poem. When you are finished, share your poem with your classmates and teacher.

Title:

Teacher Check

Write the correct answers.

6.12) A Japanese poem with three lines is known as a(n) _____.

6.13) A(n) _____ poem is one that tells a story.

6.14) A five-line poem using a specific rhythm and rhyme scheme is a(n) _____.

6.15) A(n) _____ is a seven-line poem composed of words arranged in a specific pattern.

6.16) A poetic structure that does not have a regular rhyme scheme or meter is called

_____ _____.

6.17) A(n) _____ is a poem that uses fourteen lines of iambic pentameter.

6.18) _____ _____ is a structure in which each line of a poem consists of five iambs, each containing one accented syllable.

6.19) A poem that has fourteen lines and a specific rhyme scheme and rhythmical pattern is called a(n) _____.

Choose the correct answers.

6.20) _____ This style of poetry does not tell a story, but rather, it expresses the speaker's feelings.
    A. narrative   B. lyric   C. epic   D. diamante

6.21) _____ A(n) ___ poem is a long poem that tells the story of a hero and his quest.
    A. narrative   B. lyric   C. epic   D. sonnet

6.22) _____ A(n) ___ is a poem written to praise or dedicate someone or something.
    A. epic   B. narrative   C. ode   D. limerick

6.23) _____ A ___ is a four-line segment of a poem, while a ___ is a two-line segment.
    A. quatrain; couplet   C. narrative; lyric
    B. couplet; quatrain   D. couplet; sonnet

Check   **Correct**   **Recheck**

7. MYTHOLOGY

Objective:

- Compare and contrast mythologies from various cultures.

Vocabulary:

archetype *[AHR-ki-tahyp]* – a pattern of a story that many cultures follow, such as worldwide flood

deity *[DEE-i-tee]* – a divine character in a myth; a god

myth – a story originating in a particular culture that explains some element of their world

mythology – the study of the legends or beliefs of a particular people or culture

Mythology, the study of the legends or beliefs of a particular culture, is a genre of literature that can be found in every culture known to man. A **myth** is a story that is told to explain why things are the way they are or why a culture has certain traditions or beliefs. Myths often include gods, goddesses, and heroes as the main characters and explain some element of the world. Today we regard myths as fiction, but studying them helps us to have a better understanding of the cultures from which they come.

You are likely familiar with many of the Greek gods and goddesses. Throughout this Lesson, you will read not only a Greek myth, but also an Egyptian and a Norse myth. Often, myths from different cultures have similar characters, plots, settings, and conflicts. An **archetype** is a pattern of a story that many cultures follow. Some archetype stories include the following: the creation of the world, a worldwide flood, and a war between good and evil. As you read the following myths, think about the similarities and differences between them in regard to the purpose of the myth, the roles and characteristics of the **deities** (divine characters; gods) in the myth, and the basic plot of the myth. After you read these myths, you will fill out a graphic organizer to compare and contrast them.

The first myth you will read is a Greek myth. It tells the story of Uranus and Gæa, the first two deities recognized by the Greeks. You are probably familiar with the gods Zeus, Poseidon, and Hades. This myth takes place two generations before Zeus.

The Parthenon

excerpt from
Myths and Legends of Ancient Greece and Rome
by E. M. Berens

The ancient Greeks had several different theories with regard to the origin of the world, but the generally accepted notion was that before this world came into existence, there was in its place a confused mass of shapeless elements called Chaos. These elements resolved **[set]** themselves into two widely different substances, the lighter portion of which, soaring on high, formed the sky, and constituted itself into a vast, overarching vault, which protected the firm and solid mass beneath. Thus came into being the two first great deities of the Greeks, Uranus and Ge *or* Gæa. Uranus, the more refined deity, represented the light and air of heaven, possessing the distinguishing qualities of light, heat, purity, and omnipresence, whilst Gæa, the firm, flat, life-sustaining earth, was worshipped as the great all-nourishing mother. Her many titles refer to her more or less in this character, and she appears to have been universally revered **[worshiped]** among the Greeks, there being scarcely a city in Greece which did not contain a temple in her honor.

Uranus, the heaven, was believed to have united himself in marriage with Gæa, the earth. Taken in a figurative sense, this union actually does exist. The smiles of heaven produce the flowers of earth, whereas his long-continued frowns exercise so depressing an influence upon his loving partner, that she no longer decks herself in bright and festive robes, but responds with ready sympathy to his melancholy **[sad]** mood.

The first-born child of Uranus and Gæa was Oceanus, the ocean stream, that vast expanse of ever-flowing water which encircled the earth. The ocean is formed from the rains which descend from heaven and the streams which flow from earth. By making Oceanus therefore the offspring of Uranus and Gæa, the ancients, assert that the ocean is produced by the combined influence of heaven and earth.

But Uranus, the heaven, the embodiment of light, heat, and the breath of life, produced offspring who were of a much less material nature than his son Oceanus. These other children of his were supposed to occupy the intermediate space which divided him from Gæa. Nearest to Uranus, and just beneath him, came Aether (Ether), a bright creation representing that highly rarified **[low-density]** atmosphere which immortals alone could breathe. Then followed Aër (Air), which was in close proximity to Gæa, and represented, as its name implies, the atmosphere surrounding the earth which mortals could freely breathe, and without which they would perish **[die]**.

Aether and Aër were separated from each other by divinities called Nephelae. These were their restless and wandering sisters, who existed in the form of clouds, ever floating between Aether and Aër. Gæa also produced the mountains, and Pontus (the sea). She united herself with the latter, and their offspring were the sea-deities Nereus, Thaumas, Phorcys, Ceto, and Eurybia.

Co-existent with Uranus and Gæa were two mighty powers who were also the offspring of Chaos. These were Erebus (Darkness) and Nyx (Night), who formed a striking contrast to the cheerful light of heaven and the bright smiles of earth. Erebus reigned in that mysterious world below where no ray of sunshine, no gleam of daylight, nor vestige **[trace]** of health-giving terrestrial **[earthly]** life ever appeared. Nyx, the sister of Erebus, represented Night.

Uranus was also supposed to have been united to Nyx, but only in his capacity as god of light, he being considered the source and fountain of all light, and their children were Eos (Aurora), the Dawn, and Hemera, the Daylight. Nyx again, on her side was also doubly united, having been married at some indefinite period to Erebus.

In addition to those children of heaven and earth already enumerated **[numbered]**, Uranus and Gæa produced two distinctly different races of beings called Giants and Titans. The Giants personified brute strength alone, but the Titans united to their great physical power intellectual qualifications variously developed. There were three Giants—Briareus, Cottus, and Gyges—who each possessed a hundred hands and fifty heads, and were known collectively by the name of the Hecatoncheires, which signified hundred-handed. These mighty Giants could shake the universe and produce earthquakes; it is therefore evident that they represented those active subterranean forces to which allusion has been made in the opening chapter. The Titans were twelve in number; their names were: Oceanus, Ceos, Crios, Hyperion, Iapetus, Cronus, Theia, Rhea, Themis, Mnemosyne, Phœbe, and Tethys.

Now Uranus, the chaste light of heaven, the essence of all that is bright and pleasing, held in abhorrence his crude, rough, and turbulent offspring, the Giants, and moreover feared that their great power might eventually prove hurtful to himself. He therefore hurled them into Tartarus, that portion of the lower world which served as the subterranean dungeon of the gods. In order to avenge **[take revenge on]** the oppression of her children, the Giants, Gæa instigated **[started]** a conspiracy on the part of the Titans against Uranus, which was carried to a successful issue by her son Cronus. He wounded his father, and from the blood of the wound which fell upon the earth sprang a race of monstrous beings also called Giants. Assisted by his brother-Titans, Cronus succeeded in dethroning his father, who, enraged at his defeat, cursed his rebellious son, and foretold to him a similar fate. Cronus now became invested with supreme power, and assigned to his brothers offices of distinction, subordinate only to himself. Subsequently, however, when, secure of his position, he no longer needed their assistance, he basely **[dishonorably]** repaid their former services with treachery **[betrayal]**, made war upon his brothers and faithful allies, and, assisted by the Giants, completely defeated them, sending such as resisted his all-conquering arm down into the lowest depths of Tartarus.

Now, you will read a myth from the Egyptian culture that tells the story of the god Rā. Egyptian culture is one of the oldest cultures, and Egyptian mythology has grown and changed much throughout the years.

The Literature of the Ancient Egyptians
by E. A. Walls Budge

Rā

The Legend opens with a list of the titles of Rā, the "self-created god," creator of heaven, earth, breath of life, fire, gods, men, beasts, cattle, reptiles, feathered fowl, and fish, the King of gods and men, to whom cycles of 120 years are as years, whose manifold names are unknown even by the gods. The text continues: "Isis had the form of a woman, and knew words of power, but she was disgusted with men, and she yearned for the companionship of the gods and the spirits, and she meditated and asked herself whether, supposing she had the knowledge of the Name of Rā, it was not possible to make herself as great as Rā was in heaven and on the earth?

Legends of The Gods

The Egyptians believed that at one time all the great gods and goddesses lived upon earth, and that they ruled Egypt in much the same way as the Pharaohs with whom they were more or less acquainted. They went about among men and took a real personal interest in their affairs, and, according to tradition, they spared no pains in promoting their wishes and well-being. Their rule was on the whole beneficent [kind], chiefly because in addition to their divine attributes they possessed natures, and apparently bodily constitutions that were similar to those of men. Like men also they were supposed to feel emotions and passions, and to be liable to the accidents that befell men, and to grow old, and even to die. The greatest of all the gods was Rā, and he reigned over Egypt for very many years. His reign was marked by justice and righteousness, and he was in all periods of Egyptian history regarded as the type of what a king should be.

Meanwhile Rā appeared in heaven each day upon his throne, but he had become old, and he dribbled at the mouth, and his spittle fell on the ground. One day Isis took some of the spittle and kneaded up dust in it, and made this paste into the form of a serpent with a forked tongue, so that if it struck anyone the person struck would find it impossible to escape death. This figure she placed on the path on which Rā walked as he came into heaven after his daily survey of the Two Lands (*i.e.* Egypt).

Soon after this Rā rose up, and attended by his gods he came into heaven, but as he went along the serpent drove its fangs into him. As soon as he was bitten Rā felt the living fire leaving his body, and he cried out so loudly that his voice reached the uttermost parts of heaven. The gods rushed to him in great alarm, saying, "What is the matter?" At first Rā was speechless, and found himself unable to answer, for his jaws shook, his lips trembled, and the poison continued to run through every part of his body. When he was able to regain a little strength, he told the gods that some deadly creature had bitten him, something the like of which he had never seen, something which his hand had never made. He said, "Never before have I felt such pain; there is no pain worse than this."

All the gods round about him uttered cries of lamentation, and at this moment Isis appeared. Going to Rā she said, "What is this, O divine father? What is this? Hath a serpent bitten thee? Hath something made by thee lifted up its head against thee? Verily my words of power shall overthrow it; I will make it depart in the sight of thy light." Rā then repeated to Isis the story of the incident, adding, "I am colder than water, I am hotter than fire. All my members sweat. My body quaketh. Mine eye is unsteady. I cannot look on the sky, and my face is bedewed with water as in the time of the Inundation [Great Flood]."

Then Isis said, "Father, tell me thy name, for he who can utter his own name liveth."

Rā replied, "I am the maker of heaven and earth. I knit together the mountains and whatsoever liveth on them. I made the waters. I made heaven, and the two hidden gods of the horizon, and put souls into the gods. I open my eyes, and there is light; I shut my eyes, and there is darkness. I speak the word[s], and the waters of the Nile appear. I am he whom the gods know not. I make the hours. I create

Isis

the days. I open the year. I make the river [Nile]. I create the living fire whereby works in the foundries and workshops are carried out."

Meanwhile the poison of the serpent was coursing through the veins of Rā, and the enumeration **[listing]** of his works afforded the god no relief from it. Then Isis said to Rā, "Among all the things which thou hast named to me thou hast not named thy name. Tell me thy name, and the poison shall come forth from thee."

Rā still hesitated, but the poison was burning in his blood, and the heat thereof was stronger than that of a fierce fire. At length he said, "Isis shall search me through, and my name shall come forth from my body and pass into hers." Then Rā hid himself from the gods.

When the time came for the heart of the god to pass into Isis, the goddess said to Horus, her son, "The great god shall bind himself by an oath to give us his two eyes (*i.e.* the sun and the moon)." When the great god had yielded up his name Isis pronounced the following spell: "Flow poison, come out of Rā. Eye of Horus, come out of the god, and sparkle as thou comest through his mouth. I am the worker. I make the poison to fall on the ground. The poison is conquered. Truly the name of the great god hath been taken from him. Rā liveth! The poison dieth! If the poison live Rā shall die." These were the words which Isis spoke, Isis the great lady, the Queen of the gods, who knew Rā by his own name.

The last myth you will read is a Norse myth. Norsemen means "people from the North," the region that is now referred to as Scandinavia. You may recognize elements of this story from other stories you have read, such as *The Hobbit* or *Lord of the Rings*. The following myth is a Norse creation story, which tells how our world came to be according to the ancient Norse legends.

Myths of the Norsemen
by H. A. Guerber

Once upon a time, before ever this world was made, there was neither earth nor sea, nor air, nor light, but only a great yawning gulf, full of twilight, where these things should be.

To the north of this gulf lay the Home of Mist, a dark and dreary land, out of which flowed a river of water from a spring that never ran dry. As the water in its onward course met the bitter blasts of wind from the yawning gulf, it hardened into great blocks of ice, which rolled far down into the abyss with a thunderous roar and piled themselves one on another until they formed mountains of glistening ice.

South of this gulf lay the Home of Fire, a land of burning heat, guarded by a giant with a flaming sword which, as he flashed it to and fro before the entrance, sent forth showers of sparks. And these sparks fell upon the ice-blocks and partly melted them, so that they sent up clouds of steam; and these again were frozen into hoar-frost, which filled all the space that was left in the midst of the mountains of ice.

Then one day, when the gulf was full to the very top, this great mass of frosty rime, warmed by the flames from the Home of Fire and frozen by the cold airs from the Home of Mist, came to life and became the Giant Ymir, with a living, moving body and cruel heart of ice.

Now there was as yet no tree, nor grass, nor anything that would serve for food, in this gloomy abyss. But when the Giant Ymir began to grope around for something to satisfy his hunger, he heard a sound as of some animal chewing the cud; and there among the ice-hills he saw a gigantic cow, from whose udder flowed four great streams of milk, and with this his craving was easily stilled.

But the cow was hungry also, and began to lick the salt off the blocks of ice by which she was surrounded. And presently, as she went on licking with her strong, rough tongue, a head of hair pushed itself through the melting ice. Still the cow went on licking, until she had at last melted all the icy covering and there stood fully revealed the frame of a mighty man.

Ymir looked with eyes of hatred at this being, born of snow and ice, for somehow he knew that his heart was warm and kind, and that he and his sons would always be the enemies of the evil race of the Frost Giants.

So, indeed, it came to pass. For from the sons of Ymir came a race of giants whose pleasure was to work evil on the earth; and from the Sons of the Iceman sprang the race of the gods, chief of whom was Odin, Father of All Things that ever were made; and Odin and his brothers began at once to war against the wicked Frost Giants, and most of all against the cold-hearted Ymir, whom in the end they slew.

Now when, after a hard fight, the Giant Ymir was slain, such a river of blood flowed forth from his wounds that it drowned all the rest of the Frost Giants save one, who escaped in a boat, with only his wife on board, and sailed away to the edge of the world. And from him sprang all the new race of Frost Giants, who at every

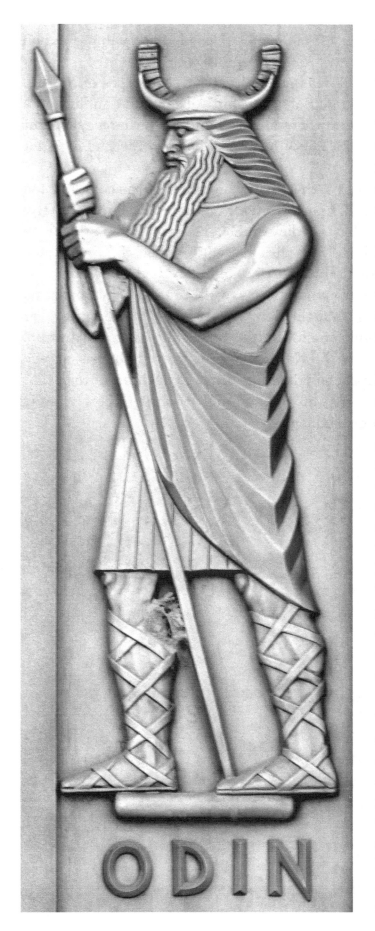

ODIN

opportunity issued from their land of twilight and desolation to harm the gods in their abode of bliss.

Now when the giants had been thus driven out, All-Father Odin set to work with his brothers to make the earth, the sea, and the sky; and these they fashioned out of the great body of the Giant Ymir.

Out of his flesh they formed Midgard, the earth, which lay in the center of the gulf; and all round it they planted his eyebrows to make a high fence which should defend it from the race of giants.

With his bones they made the lofty hills, with his teeth the cliffs, and his thick curly hair took root and became trees, bushes, and the green grass. With his blood they made the ocean, and his great skull, poised aloft, became the arching sky. Just below this they scattered his brains, and made of them the heavy grey clouds that lie between earth and heaven. The sky itself was held in place by four strong dwarfs, who support it on their broad shoulders as they stand east and west and south and north.

The next thing was to give light to the new-made world. So the gods caught sparks from the Home of Fire and set them in the sky for stars; and they took the living flame and made of it the sun and moon, which they placed in chariots of gold, and harnessed to them beautiful horses, with flowing manes of gold and silver. Before the horses of the sun, they placed a mighty shield to protect them from its hot rays; but the swift moon steeds needed no such protection from its gentle heat.

And now all was ready save that there was no one to drive the horses of the sun and moon. This task was given to Mani and Sol, the beautiful son and daughter of a giant; and these fair charioteers drive their fleet steeds along the paths marked out by the gods, and not only give light to the earth but mark out months and days for the sons of men.

Then All-Father Odin called forth Night, the gloomy daughter of the cold-hearted giant folk, and set her to drive the dark chariot drawn by the black horse, Frosty-Mane, from whose long wavy hair the drops of dew and hoar-frost fall upon the earth below. After her drove her radiant son, Day, with his white steed Shining-Mane, from whom the bright beams of daylight shine forth to gladden the hearts of men.

But the wicked giants were very angry when they saw all these good things; and they set in the sky two hungry wolves, that the fierce, grey creatures might forever pursue the sun and moon, and devour them, and so bring all things to an end. Sometimes, indeed, or so say the men of the North, the grey wolves almost succeed in swallowing sun or moon; and then the earth children make such an uproar that the fierce beasts drop their prey in fear. And the sun and moon flee more rapidly than before, still pursued by the hungry monsters.

And now that this pleasant Midgard was made, the gods determined to satisfy their desire for an abode where they might rest and enjoy themselves in their hours of ease. They chose a suitable place far above the earth, on the other side of the great river which flowed from the Home of Mist where the giants dwelt, and here they made for their abode Asgard, wherein they dwelt in peace and happiness, and from whence they could look down upon the sons of men.

From Asgard to Midgard they built a beautiful bridge of many colors, to which men gave the name of Rainbow Bridge, and up and down which the gods could pass on their journeys to and from the earth.

Meantime, no human creature lived upon the earth, and the giants dared not cross its borders for fear

of the gods. But one of them, clad in eagles' plumes **[feathers]**, always sat at the north side of Midgard, and, whenever he raised his arms and let them fall again, an icy blast rushed forth from the Mist Home and nipped all the pleasant things of earth with its cruel breath. In due time the earth was no longer without life, for the ground brought forth thousands of tiny creatures, which crawled about and showed signs of great intelligence. And when the gods examined these little people closely, they found that they were of two kinds.

Some were ugly, misshapen, and cunning-faced, with great heads, small bodies, long arms and feet. These they called Trolls or Dwarfs or Gnomes, and sent them to live underground, threatening to turn them into stone should they appear in the daytime. And this is why the trolls spend all their time in the hidden parts of the earth, digging for gold and silver and precious stones, and hiding their spoil away in secret holes and corners. Sometimes they blow their tiny fires and set to work to make all kinds of wonderful things from this buried treasure; and that is what they are doing when, if one listens very hard on the mountains and hills of the Northland, a sound of tap-tap-tapping is heard far underneath the ground.

The other small earth creatures were very fair and light and slender, kindly of heart, and full of goodwill. These the gods called Fairies or Elves, and gave to them a charming place called Elfland in which to dwell. Elfland lies between Asgard and Midgard, and since all fairies have wings they can easily flit down to the earth to play with the butterflies, teach the young birds to sing, water the flowers, or dance in the moonlight round a fairy ring.

Last of all, the gods made a man and woman to dwell in fair Midgard; and this is the manner of their creation.

All-Father Odin was walking with his brothers in Midgard where, by the seashore, they found growing two trees, an ash and an elm. Odin took these trees and breathed on them, whereupon a wonderful transformation took place. Where the trees had stood, there were a living man and woman, but they were stupid, pale, and speechless, until Hœnir, the god of Light, touched their fore-heads and gave them sense and wisdom; and Loki, the Fire-god, smoothed their faces, giving them bright colour and warm blood, and the power to speak and see and hear. It only remained that they should be named, and they were called Ask and Embla, the names of the trees from which they had been formed. From these two people sprang all the race of men which lives upon this earth.

And now All-Father Odin completed his work by planting the Tree of Life.

This immense tree had its roots in Asgard and Midgard and the Mist Land; and it grew to such a marvelous height that the highest bough, the Bough of Peace, hung over the Hall of Odin on the heights of Asgard; and the other branches overshadowed both Midgard and the Mist Land. On the top of the Peace Bough was perched a mighty eagle, and ever a falcon sat between his eyes, and kept watch on all that happened in the world below, that he might tell to Odin what he saw.

The leaves of the Tree of Life were ever green and fair, despite the dragon which, aided by countless serpents, gnawed perpetually at its roots, in order that they might kill the Tree of Life and thus bring about the destruction of the gods.

Up and down the branches of the tree scampered the squirrel, Ratatosk, a malicious little creature, whose one amusement it was to make mischief by repeating to the eagle the rude remarks of the dragon, and to the dragon those of the eagle, in the hope that one day he might see them in actual conflict.

Near the roots of the Tree of life is a sacred well of sweet water from which the three Weird Sisters, who know all that shall come to pass, sprinkle the tree and keep it fresh and green. And the water, as it trickles down from the leaves, falls as drops of honey on the earth, and the bees take it for their food.

Close to this sacred well is the Council Hall of the gods, to which every morning they rode, over the Rainbow Bridge, to converse together.

And this is the end of the tale of How All Things began.

Complete the graphic organizer, based on the myths in this Lesson.

	Greek Myth	Egyptian Myth	Norse Myth
Purpose of the Myth	7.1)	7.2)	7.3)
Chief Deities	7.4)	7.5)	7.6)
Brief Summary of Myth	7.7)	7.8)	7.9)

7.10) What is one thing the Greek and the Norse myths have in common? _____

_____

_____

7.11) What is one difference between the deities in the Egyptian and the Norse myths? _____

_____

_____

_____

Fill in the blanks using words from the box below.

Rā	Isis	Ymir	mythology
archetype	Midgard	Odin	Uranus
Gæa	Cronus	deity	myths

7.12) _____ is the Norse name for the home of mankind.

7.13) To the Greeks, _____ represented the light of heaven.

7.14) _____ was successful in overthrowing his father.

7.15) In the Egyptian culture, the creator god was bitten by a snake and turned to _____ for help.

7.16) _____ is the name of the creator god in Egyptian culture.

7.17) The name of the frost-giant is _____, in Norse culture.

7.18) _____ was the earth in Greek mythology.

7.19) In Norse culture, _____ is the Father of All Things.

7.20) _____ is the study of the legends or beliefs of a particular people or culture.

7.21) A pattern of a story that many cultures follow, such as a worldwide flood, is called a(n) _____.

7.22) A(n) _____ is the name for a divine character in a myth, also called a god.

7.23) Various cultures used _____ as stories to explain some elements of their world.

Check   **Correct**   **Recheck**

8. "A RETRIEVED REFORMATION"

Objective:

- Apply knowledge of literary terms to a fictional work.

Now that you have learned the elements of literature throughout this Unit, you will practice what you have learned by reading a story and applying your knowledge of literary terms. The fictional short story, "A Retrieved Reformation" by O. Henry, tells the story of a man named Jimmy Valentine who was in prison for being a safe cracker. The story begins as he is being released from prison.

Before you begin reading, think about the title—"A Retrieved Reformation." The word

retrieved means "recovered" or "reclaimed," and the word *reformation* means "positive change." How could this title apply to the story?

As you read, try to get a sense of the characters' traits and the motivations for their actions. Think about the elements of literature— plot, setting, conflict, characterization—as you read the story. The definitions of some words are provided for you. The paragraph numbers will help you in answering the questions at the end of the selection.

¹ A guard came to the prison shoe-shop, where Jimmy Valentine was assiduously **[diligently]** stitching uppers, and escorted him to the front office. There the warden handed Jimmy his pardon, which had been signed that morning by the governor. Jimmy took it in a tired kind of way. He had served nearly ten months of a four year sentence. He had expected to stay only about three months, at the longest. When a man with as many friends on the outside as Jimmy Valentine had is received in the "stir" it is hardly worthwhile to cut his hair.

² "Now, Valentine," said the warden, "you'll go out in the morning. Brace up, and make a man of yourself. You're not a bad fellow at heart. Stop cracking safes, and live straight."

³ "Me?" said Jimmy, in surprise. "Why, I never cracked a safe in my life."

⁴ "Oh, no," laughed the warden. "Of course not. Let's see, now. How was it you happened to get sent up on that Springfield job? Was it because you wouldn't prove an alibi for fear of compromising somebody in extremely high-toned society? Or was it simply a case of a mean old jury that had it in for you? It's always one or the other with you innocent victims."

⁵ "Me?" said Jimmy, still blankly virtuous. "Why, warden, I never was in Springfield in my life!"

⁶ "Take him back, Cronin!" said the warden, "and fix him up with outgoing clothes. Unlock him at seven in the morning, and let him come to the bull-pen. Better think over my advice, Valentine."

⁷ At a quarter past seven on the next morning Jimmy stood in the warden's outer office. He had on a suit of the villainously **[unpleasantly]** fitting, ready-made clothes and a pair of the stiff, squeaky shoes that the state furnishes to its discharged compulsory **[forced]** guests.

⁸ The clerk handed him a railroad ticket and the five-dollar bill with which the law expected him to rehabilitate **[restore]** himself into good citizenship and prosperity. The warden gave him a cigar, and shook hands. Valentine, 9762, was chronicled on the books, "Pardoned by Governor," and Mr. James Valentine walked out into the sunshine. **[*Pardon* means to release from the penalty of an offense]**

***

⁹ A week after the release of Valentine, 9762, there was a neat job of safe-burglary done in Richmond, Indiana, with no clue to the author. A scant eight hundred dollars was all that was secured. Two weeks after that a patented, improved, burglar-proof safe in Logansport was opened like a cheese to the tune of fifteen hundred dollars, currency; securities and silver untouched. That began to interest the rogue-catchers **[criminal-catchers]**. Then an old-fashioned bank-safe in Jefferson City became active and threw out of its crater an eruption of bank-notes amounting to five thousand dollars. The losses were now high enough to bring the matter up into Ben Price's class of work. By comparing notes, a remarkable similarity in the methods of the burglaries was noticed. Ben Price investigated the scenes of the robberies, and was heard to remark:

¹⁰ "That's Dandy Jim Valentine's autograph. He's resumed business. Look at that combination knob—jerked out as easy as pulling up a radish in wet weather. He's got the only clamps that can do it. And look how clean those tumblers were punched out! Jimmy never has to drill but one hole. Yes, I guess I want Mr. Valentine. He'll do his bit next time without any short-time or clemency foolishness."

¹¹ Ben Price knew Jimmy's habits. He had learned them while working up the Springfield case. Long jumps, quick get-aways, no confederates **[partners]**, and a taste for good society—these ways had helped Mr. Valentine to become noted as a successful dodger of retribution **[punishment]**. It was given out that Ben Price had

taken up the trail of the elusive cracksman, and other people with burglar-proof safes felt more at ease.

¹² One afternoon Jimmy Valentine and his suit-case climbed out of the mail-hack in Elmore, a little town five miles off the railroad down in the black-jack country of Arkansas. Jimmy, looking like an athletic young senior just home from college, went down the board side-walk toward the hotel.

¹³ A young lady crossed the street, passed him at the corner and entered a door over which was the sign, "The Elmore Bank." Jimmy Valentine looked into her eyes, forgot what he was, and became another man. She lowered her eyes and colored slightly. Young men of Jimmy's style and looks were scarce in Elmore.

¹⁴ Jimmy collared a boy that was loafing on the steps of the bank as if he were one of the stockholders, and began to ask him questions about the town, feeding him dimes at intervals. By and by the young lady came out, looking royally unconscious of the young man with the suit-case, and went her way.

¹⁵ "Isn't that young lady Polly Simpson?" asked Jimmy, with specious guile.

¹⁶ "Naw," said the boy. "She's Annabel Adams. Her pa owns this bank. What'd you come to Elmore for? Is that a gold watch-chain? I'm going to get a bulldog. Got any more dimes?"

¹⁷ Jimmy went to the Planters' Hotel, registered as Ralph D. Spencer, and engaged a room. He leaned on the desk and declared his platform to the clerk. He said he had come to Elmore to look for a location to go into business. How was the shoe business, now, in the town? He had thought of the shoe business. Was there an opening?

¹⁸ The clerk was impressed by the clothes and manner of Jimmy. He, himself, was something of a pattern of fashion to the thinly gilded youth of Elmore, but he now perceived his shortcomings. While trying to figure out Jimmy's manner of tying his four-in-hand he cordially gave information.

¹⁹ Yes, there ought to be a good opening in the shoe line. There wasn't an exclusive shoe-store in the place. The dry-goods and general stores handled them. Business in all lines was fairly good. Hoped Mr. Spencer would decide to locate in Elmore. He would find it a pleasant town to live in, and the people very sociable.

20 Mr. Spencer thought he would stop over in the town a few days and look over the situation. No, the clerk needn't call the boy. He would carry up his suitcase, himself; it was rather heavy.

21 Mr. Ralph Spencer, the phoenix that arose from Jimmy Valentine's ashes— ashes left by the flame of a sudden and alterative attack of love—remained in Elmore, and prospered. He opened a shoe-store and secured a good run of trade. **[A phoenix is a mythical bird that was believed to have the ability to be reborn from its own ashes.]**

22 Socially he was also a success, and made many friends. And he accomplished the wish of his heart. He met Miss Annabel Adams, and became more and more captivated by her charms.

23 At the end of a year the situation of Mr. Ralph Spencer was this: he had won the respect of the community, his shoe-store was flourishing, and he and Annabel were engaged to be married in two weeks. Mr. Adams, the typical, plodding, country banker, approved of Spencer. Annabel's pride in him almost equalled her affection. He was as much at home in the family of Mr. Adams and that of Annabel's married sister as if he were already a member.

24 One day Jimmy sat down in his room and wrote this letter, which he mailed to the safe address of one of his old friends in St. Louis:

25

Dear Old Pal

I want you to be at Sullivan's place, in Little Rock, next Wednesday night, at nine o'clock. I want you to wind up some little matters for me. And, also, I want to make you a present of my kit of tools. I know you'll be glad to get them—you couldn't duplicate the lot for a thousand dollars. Say, Billy, I've quit the old business—a year ago. I've got a nice store. I'm making an honest living, and I'm going to marry the finest girl on earth two weeks from now. It's the only life, Billy—the straight one. I wouldn't touch a dollar of another man's money now for a million. After I get married I'm going to sell out and go West, where there won't be so much danger of having old scores brought up against me. I tell you, Billy, she's an angel. She believes in me; and I wouldn't do another crooked thing for the whole world. Be sure to be at Sully's, for I must see you. I'll bring along the tools with me.

Your old friend,

Jimmy.

26 On the Monday night after Jimmy wrote this letter, Ben Price jogged unobtrusively **[without being noticed]** into Elmore in a livery buggy. He lounged about town in

his quiet way until he found out what he wanted to know. From the drug-store across the street from Spencer's shoe-store he got a good look at Ralph D. Spencer.

27 "Going to marry the banker's daughter are you, Jimmy?" said Ben to himself, softly. "Well, I don't know!"

28 The next morning Jimmy took breakfast at the Adamses. He was going to Little Rock that day to order his wedding-suit and buy something nice for Annabel. That would be the first time he had left town since he came to Elmore. It had been more than a year now since those last professional "jobs," and he thought he could safely venture out.

29 After breakfast quite a family party went downtown together—Mr. Adams, Annabel, Jimmy, and Annabel's married sister with her two little girls, aged five and nine. They came by the hotel where Jimmy still boarded, and he ran up to his room and brought along his suit-case. Then they went on to the bank. There stood Jimmy's horse and buggy and Dolph Gibson, who was going to drive him over to the railroad station.

30 All went inside the high, carved oak railings into the banking-room—Jimmy included, for Mr. Adams's future son-in-law was welcome anywhere. The clerks were pleased to be greeted by the good-looking, agreeable young man who was going to marry Miss Annabel. Jimmy set his suit-case down. Annabel, whose heart was bubbling with happiness and lively youth, put on Jimmy's hat, and picked up the suit-case. "Wouldn't I make a nice drummer?" said Annabel. "My! Ralph, how heavy it is? Feels like it was full of gold bricks."

31 "Lot of nickel-plated shoe-horns in there," said Jimmy, coolly, "that I'm going to return. Thought I'd save express charges by taking them up. I'm getting awfully economical."

32 The Elmore Bank had just put in a new safe and vault. Mr. Adams was very proud of it, and insisted on an inspection by everyone. The vault was a small one, but it had a new, patented door. It fastened with three solid steel bolts thrown simultaneously with a single handle, and had a time-lock. Mr. Adams beamingly explained its workings to Mr. Spencer, who showed a courteous but not too intelligent interest.

Vault door

The two children, May and Agatha, were delighted by the shining metal and funny clock and knobs.

33 While they were thus engaged Ben Price sauntered in and leaned on his elbow, looking casually inside between the railings. He told the teller that he didn't want anything; he was just waiting for a man he knew.

34 Suddenly there was a scream or two from the women, and a commotion. Unperceived by the elders, May, the nine-year-old girl, in a spirit of play, had shut Agatha

in the vault. She had then shot the bolts and turned the knob of the combination as she had seen Mr. Adams do.

35 The old banker sprang to the handle and tugged at it for a moment. "The door can't be opened," he groaned. "The clock hasn't been wound nor the combination set."

36 Agatha's mother screamed again, hysterically.

37 "Hush!" said Mr. Adams, raising his trembling hand. "All be quite for a moment. Agatha!" he called as loudly as he could. "Listen to me." During the following silence they could just hear the faint sound of the child wildly shrieking in the dark vault in a panic of terror.

38 "My precious darling!" wailed the mother. "She will die of fright! Open the door! Oh, break it open! Can't you men do something?"

39 "There isn't a man nearer than Little Rock who can open that door," said Mr. Adams, in a shaky voice. "My God! Spencer, what shall we do? That child—she can't stand it long in there. There isn't enough air, and, besides, she'll go into convulsions from fright."

40 Agatha's mother, frantic now, beat the door of the vault with her hands. Somebody wildly suggested dynamite. Annabel turned to Jimmy, her large eyes full of anguish, but not yet despairing. To a woman nothing seems quite impossible to the powers of the man she worships.

41 "Can't you do something, Ralph—*try*, won't you?"

42 He looked at her with a queer, soft smile on his lips and in his keen eyes.

43 "Annabel," he said, "give me that rose you are wearing, will you?"

44 Hardly believing that she heard him aright, she unpinned the bud from the bosom of her dress, and placed it in his hand. Jimmy stuffed it into his vest-pocket, threw off his coat and pulled up his shirt-sleeves. With that act Ralph D. Spencer passed away and Jimmy Valentine took his place.

45 "Get away from the door, all of you," he commanded, shortly.

46 He set his suit-case on the table, and opened it out flat. From that time on he seemed to be unconscious of the presence of anyone else. He laid out the shining, queer implements swiftly and orderly, whistling softly to himself as he always did when at work. In a deep silence and immovable, the others watched him as if under a spell.

47 In a minute Jimmy's pet drill was biting smoothly into the steel door. In ten minutes—breaking his own burglarious record—he threw back the bolts and opened the door.

48 Agatha, almost collapsed, but safe, was gathered into her mother's arms.

49 Jimmy Valentine put on his coat, and walked outside the railings towards the front door. As he went he thought he heard a far-away voice that he once knew call "Ralph!" But he never hesitated.

50 At the door a big man stood somewhat in his way.

51 "Hello, Ben!" said Jimmy, still with his strange smile. "Got around at last, have you? Well, let's go. I don't know that it makes much difference, now."

⁵² And then Ben Price acted rather strangely.

⁵³ "Guess you're mistaken, Mr. Spencer," he said. "Don't believe I recognize you. Your buggy's waiting for you, ain't it?"

⁵⁴ And Ben Price turned and strolled down the street.

 # Review

Choose the correct answers.

8.1) _____ What inference can you make from paragraphs 2–6?
    A. Jimmy really believes he is innocent.
    B. Jimmy is using verbal irony, or sarcasm, by saying he has never cracked a safe.
    C. The warden is trying to frame Jimmy.
    D. The warden believes that Jimmy is innocent.

8.2) _____ Putting together the clues in paragraphs 1 and 8, how did Jimmy get out of jail after serving only ten months of a four-year sentence?
    A. Jimmy has influential "friends" who got the governor to pardon him.
    B. He was proven to be innocent.
    C. He convinced the warden to let him out early.
    D. Jimmy's friends helped him plan an elaborate escape from prison.

8.3) _____ What inference can you make from paragraph 9?
    A. Jimmy Valentine has reformed his ways.
    B. Someone else has taken Jimmy's place as expert safecracker.
    C. Ben Price has given up searching for Jimmy Valentine.
    D. Jimmy has resumed his old ways of safecracking.

8.4) _____ What does the following sentence from paragraph 13 suggest? *Jimmy Valentine looked into her eyes, forgot what he was, and became another man.*
    A. Jimmy experienced memory loss.
    B. One look at Annabel has made Jimmy forget his life of crime and desire to change his ways.
    C. Jimmy changed his outward appearance so that he wouldn't get caught.
    D. Annabel knew Jimmy was a safecracker, but she convinced him to reform his ways.

8.5) _____ Interpret the meaning of paragraphs 20–21.
    A. Jimmy Valentine's life has been completely transformed because he fell in love.
    B. Ralph Spencer took Jimmy's place as a safecracker.
    C. Jimmy is living a double life as a shoe repairman by day and a safecracker by night.
    D. Annabel knows of Jimmy's past but believes he has truly changed.

8.6) _____ Reread the letter Jimmy sends to one of his old friends, Billy (paragraph 25). How do you know Jimmy's change is sincere?
A. He wants to cut off all ties with all his friends from his old life.
B. He is going to tell Annabel the truth and turn himself in.
C. He now owns a shoe store and is making an honest living.
D. He says he is going to give all his safecracking tools to Billy.

8.7) _____ What is the primary conflict of this story?
A. Jimmy has resumed his old life of safecracking and does not want to get caught.
B. Jimmy has changed his ways but must avoid being caught by Ben Price in order to keep his old life a secret.
C. Jimmy tries to make Annabel fall in love with him.
D. Jimmy must convince Annabel that he has left his old life behind.

8.8) _____ What is the climax of this story?
A. Jimmy continues to crack safes after he is released from prison.
B. Jimmy meets Annabel and decides to change his ways.
C. Jimmy must decide whether to crack the safe to save Agatha or to keep his old life a secret.
D. Ben Price finally catches Jimmy Valentine.

8.9) _____ Interpret the meaning of the figurative expression in this sentence in paragraph 44.
With that act Ralph D. Spencer passed away and Jimmy Valentine took his place.
A. Ralph Spencer literally died.
B. Jimmy stopped pretending he was someone else.
C. Jimmy went back to his old criminal ways of safecracking and stealing money.
D. Jimmy officially changed his name from Ralph D. Spencer back to Jimmy Valentine.

8.10) _____ How does Jimmy show a true change of character at the end of the story?
A. He asks Annabel to marry him.
B. He risks everything he has—his new life and identity—to save someone's life.
C. He turns himself in and allows Ben Price to catch him.
D. He refuses to crack the safe and return to his old life of crime.

8.11) _____ How is the conflict of the story resolved?
A. Even though Jimmy reveals his old life and identity, Ben Price lets Jimmy go.
B. Ben Price is successful in catching Jimmy.
C. Jimmy gets rid of his safe-cracking tools to cut all ties with his old life.
D. Annabel marries Jimmy and they move out West.

8.12) _____ What effect does the point of view have on the story?
   A. It is first-person, allowing the reader to understand the story from Jimmy's perspective.
   B. It is third-person objective, allowing the reader to see Jimmy's change of character from the outside.
   C. It is third-person limited, allowing the reader to understand Jimmy's inner struggle to resist his old lifestyle.
   D. It is third-person omniscient, allowing the reader to understand the thoughts and feelings of all characters.

8.13) _____ Based on the characters' qualities and the resolution of the conflict, which statement best represents the theme of the story?
   A. It is impossible for a criminal to reform his character.
   B. Love is not a strong enough motivation for someone to truly change.
   C. It is wrong to pretend to be someone you are not.
   D. Sometimes an act of true selflessness can redeem a person from former acts of selfishness.

Check   Correct   Recheck

Write the answer to this question in at least three complete sentences.

8.14) In Lesson 3, you read "After Twenty Years," also by O. Henry. In this story, the plainclothes officer tells "Silky" Bob that twenty years "sometimes changes a good man into a bad one," indicating that Bob had taken on the lifestyle of a criminal. How does the theme of "After Twenty Years" relate to the theme of "A Retrieved Reformation"? Are the themes similar or different? Explain. (If you need to, review the story from Lesson 3.) _____

_____

_____

_____

_____

_____

_____

_____

 **Teacher Check** ☐

(Each answer, 4 points)
Match the poetry terms with the descriptions.

3.01) _____ couplet

3.02) _____ diamante

3.03) _____ epic poem

3.04) _____ free verse

3.05) _____ iambic pentameter

3.06) _____ quatrain

3.07) _____ sonnet

3.08) _____ ode

A. a line of poetry that contains five groups of two syllables, with one accented syllable in each group; commonly used in the sonnet

B. a seven-line poem composed of words arranged in a specific pattern

C. a lyric poem written to praise someone or something

D. a group of four lines of poetry

E. a group of two lines of poetry

F. a long narrative poem that tells about a hero's quest

G. a fourteen-line poem that has a specific rhyme scheme and meter

H. a poem that does not have a specific rhyme scheme or meter

Identify the correct type of poem for each example using words from the box below.

haiku	limerick	lyric	narrative

3.09) _____

Listen my children and you shall hear
Of the midnight ride of Paul Revere,
On the eighteenth of April, in Seventy-five;
Hardly a man is now alive
Who remembers that famous day and year.

3.010) _____

There was an Old Man in a Tree,
Whose Whiskers were lovely to see;
But the Birds of the Air
Pluck'd them perfectly bare
To make themselves Nests in that Tree.

3.011) _____

Pointed white object
soars to the front of the room—
teacher looks enraged.

3.012) _____

If I can stop one heart from breaking,
I shall not live in vain;
If I can ease one life the aching,
Or cool one pain,
Or help one fainting robin
Unto his nest again,
I shall not live in vain.

Choose the correct answers.

3.013) _____ A pattern of a story, such as a worldwide flood, that many cultures follow is called
a(n) ___.
A. deity   B. sonnet   C. lyric   D. archetype

3.014) _____ The study of the legends and beliefs of a particular people or culture is called ___.
A. mythology   B. archetype   C. deity   D. lyric

3.015) _____ The gods or divine characters in myths are called ___.
A. myths   B. archetypes   C. giants   D. deities

3.016) _____ What was the main purpose of myths in a culture, traditionally?
A. to provide recreation
B. to explain how the world came to be or to explain other natural elements
C. to prove why the people of that culture were better than people of other cultures
D. to provide topics of conversation during feasts

(Circle) **the correct culture for each mythical character.**

3.017) **Rā**   Greek   Norse   Egyptian

3.018) **Ymir**   Greek   Norse   Egyptian

3.019) **Odin**   Greek   Norse   Egyptian

3.020) **Uranus**   Greek   Norse   Egyptian

3.021) **Isis**   Greek   Norse   Egyptian

Match the words with the descriptions.

3.022) _____ narrative

3.023) _____ haiku

3.024) _____ limerick

3.025) _____ lyric

A. a three-line poem whose first and third lines have five syllables
and whose second line has seven syllables
B. a poem that expresses a speaker's feelings
C. a poem that tells a story
D. a humerous, five-line poem with specific rhyme scheme and meter

Check   Correct   Recheck

STOP and prepare for the Unit Practice Test.
- Review the Objectives and Vocabulary for each Lesson.
- Reread each Lesson and its corresponding questions.
- Relearn each Lesson that you still do not understand.
- Review the Quizzes.

(Each answer, 2.5 points)
Read the poem; then choose the correct answers.

"Wisdom"
by Sara Teasdale

It was a night of early spring,
The winter-sleep was scarcely broken;
Around us shadows and the wind
Listened for what was never spoken.

Though half a score of years are gone,
Spring comes as sharply now as then—
But if we had it all to do
It would be done the same again.

It was a spring that never came;
But we have lived enough to know
That what we never have, remains;
It is the things we have that go.

1) _____ Which line contains personification?
   A. It was a night of early spring
   B. Listened for what was never spoken
   C. Spring comes as sharply now as then
   D. It would be done the same again

2) _____ What is the rhyme scheme of this poem?
   A. ABAB   B. ABBA   C. ABCB   D. ABCD

3) _____ Which lines from the poem best represent the theme of the poem?
   A. Though half a score of years are gone, / Spring comes as sharply now as then—
   B. It was a night of early spring, / The winter-sleep was scarcely broken;
   C. But if we had it all to do / It would be done the same again.
   D. That what we never have, remains; / It is the things we have that go.

4) _____ The words *spring*, *sleep*, *scarcely*, *shadows*, and *spoken* in the first stanza create ___.
   A. imagery   B. alliteration   C. onomatopoeia   D. rhyme

Match the literary terms with the descriptions.

5) _____ point of view

6) _____ figurative language

7) _____ irony

8) _____ symbol

9) _____ meter

10) _____ hyperbole

11) _____ extended metaphor

12) _____ conflict

13) _____ couplet

A. the rhythmical pattern of stressed and unstressed syllables

B. the literal message is the opposite of the reader's expectation

C. an exaggerated statement

D. words and phrases that are not meant to be taken literally

E. a group of two lines of poetry

F. a comparison that is implied or stated throughout a poem

G. something that stands for something else

H. the problem in a literary work

I. the perspective from which a story is told

Read the poem; then choose the correct answers.

"The Bee"
by Emily Dickinson

Like trains of cars on tracks of plush
I hear the level bee:
A jar across the flowers goes,
Their velvet masonry

Withstands until the sweet assault
Their chivalry consumes,
While he, victorious, tilts away
To vanquish other blooms.

His feet are shod with gauze,
His helmet is of gold;
His breastplate, a single onyx
With chrysoprase, inlaid.

His labor is a chant,
His idleness a tune;
Oh, for a bee's experience
Of clovers and of noon!

---

14) _____ The first two lines create ___.
    A. personification, comparing the bee to a train.
    B. a metaphor, stating that the bee is a train.
    C. a simile, comparing the bee to train cars.
    D. a hyperbole, exaggerating the movements of the bee.

15) _____ Words like *chivalry*, *vanquish*, *feet . . . shod*, *helmet*, and *breastplate* create a(n) ___, suggesting the comparison between the bee and a knight in armor.
    A. metaphor   B. simile   C. hyperbole   D. irony

16) _____ Which line creates imagery that appeals to the sense of touch?
    A. A jar across the flower goes
    B. I hear the level bee
    C. Their velvet masonry
    D. Withstands until the sweet assault

Fill in the blanks using words from the box below.

climax	simile	one	all
diamante	epic poem	free verse	haiku
limerick	lyric	narrative	ode
quatrain	sonnet	couplet	free verse
mythology	theme	alliteration	

17) A(n) _____ poem is one that tells a story.

18) A group of four lines of poetry is called a(n) _____.

19) A poem written to praise or dedicate a person or place is a(n) _____.

20) The poem "Upstream" by Carl Sandburg does not contain a rhyme scheme or rhythmical pattern, so it is written in _____ form.

21) A type of poem that tells the story of a hero and his quest is a(n) _____.

22) Iambic pentameter is the rhythmical pattern commonly used in the _____.

23) A(n) _____ poem does not tell a story, but rather, it expresses the feelings of the speaker.

24) A humorous, five-line poem that has a specific rhyme scheme and meter is called a(n) _____.

25) A three-line poem whose first and third lines have five syllables and whose second line has seven syllables would be a(n) _____.

26) A(n) _____ is a seven-line poem composed of words arranged in a specific shape.

27) _____ is a style of poetry that does not have a specific rhyme scheme or meter.

28) A(n) _____ is a comparison using "like" or "as."

29) A story reaches its peak at the _____ of a story.

30) In third-person omniscience, the narrator reveals the thoughts of _____ of the characters.

31) _____ is the study of the legends and beliefs of a particular people or culture.

32) A(n) _____ is the message or insight revealed by a literary work.

33) _____ is the repetition of beginning sounds in words that are close together.

Choose the correct answers.

34) _____ A pattern of a story, such as a worldwide flood, that many cultures follow is called a(n) ___.
   A. narrative   B. archetype   C. deity   D. creation myth

35) _____ The point of view in which one of the characters is the narrator is ___.
   A. first-person   C. third-person limited
   B. third-person objective   D. third-person omniscient

36) _____ In the ___ point of view, the narrator tells the story from the perspective of an outsider.
   A. subjective   C. first-person
   B. objective   D. third-person limited

37) _____ Which of the following words best defines theme?
   A. plot   B. genre   C. inference   D. message

38) _____ The gods in myths, such as Rā, Isis, and Odin, are called ___.
   A. archetypes   B. creators   C. deities   D. heroes

39) _____ The main purpose of a(n) ___ is to explain elements of the natural world.
   A. epic   B. archetype   C. ode   D. myth

40) _____ The creator-god in Egyptian culture is ___.
   A. Rā   B. Odin   C. Isis   D. Uranus

Check   **Correct**   **Recheck**

You must now prepare for the Unit Test.
- Review the Objectives and Vocabulary for each Lesson.
- Reread each Lesson and its corresponding questions.
- Review and study the Quizzes and Unit Practice Test.

When you are ready, turn in your Unit and request your Unit Test.